Cost and Budget Analysis

Cost and
Budget Analysis

JOHN DEARDEN

LECTURER IN BUSINESS ADMINISTRATION
GRADUATE SCHOOL OF BUSINESS ADMINISTRATION
HARVARD UNIVERSITY

Prentice-Hall, Inc.
ENGLEWOOD CLIFFS, N. J.   1962

Preface

This book is concerned with the financial information that management needs for making short-term operating decisions. (A short-term decision is one that will be effective for a period of one year or less.) Specifically, the book covers cost accounting, cost analysis, and budgetary control. It does not cover capital investment analysis, long-term profit planning, or decentralized profit control techniques, because they relate to long-run operating decisions.

The purpose of internal accounting and financial data is to provide management with information for making intelligent decisions. The effectiveness of a cost accounting and control system can be measured in terms of the usefulness of the information it provides to management. Throughout the book, the criterion that has been used to evaluate cost accounting and budgeting techniques has been the value to management of the data that they produce. In nearly every case, the questions to be answered are: "What information does management need for decision making?" and "Which accounting (or budget) technique provides this information best?"

The intention of the author has not been to write a complete textbook for a course in cost analysis and budgetary control. Rather, the book has been designed for three areas:

First, it has been written for use as a text supplement for a "case" course in cost accounting and budgeting. (The author is presently using it for this purpose at the Harvard Graduate School of Business Administration.)

Second, it can be used as a supplementary textbook in a course in cost accounting, budgeting, or industrial management.

Third, it is designed for the industrial accountant, the budget analyst, and the consultant. The book results from a dozen years' experience in industry and consulting. The author would like to think that this experience is useful to the men who are currently working in the cost accounting and budgetary control field.

The book assumes some knowledge of accounting. A course in "managerial accounting" or a course in elementary accounting plus an acquaintance with cost accounting should be sufficient to understand any part of this book. (The first chapter provides a review of the main elements ot cost accounting.) Those aspects of cost accounting of interest primarily to the accountant, particularly the record-keeping side of cost accounting, are avoided as much as possible. It has been the author's object to write the budgetary control part of the book (Chapters 6, 7, and 8) so that it can be understood by someone with practically no accounting background but with an understanding of business procedures.

In formulating the ideas expressed in this book, the author has been assisted by many people. He is particularly indebted to the people with whom he worked in the Controller's Office of the Ford Motor Company. He is also indebted to many of the faculty of the Harvard Graduate School of Business Administration for the help, encouragement, and stimulation that they have given him. Especially, he would like to mention Professors Clarence Nickerson and Earl Bennett. Teaching a course in Industrial Accounting, which they developed, was the final impetus for this book. In the process of teaching this course, the author has used both text and cases that they have written. As a result, many of the ideas expressed in this book were first suggested by their material. Acknowledgment is also made to Professors Dennis Gordon, of the College of Business Administration, the University of Akron, and David Solomons, of Wharton School of Finance & Commerce, University of Pennsylvania, who read the manuscript and made many valuable suggestions.

J.D.

To Helen-Marie

Contents

8. Budgetary Control (Part III)—Continued

tion volumes are equal; Profit budget reports when sales and production volumes are different; The profit budget and the forecast. Summary.

9. Profit Analysis   *141*

Differential Cost Analysis: Differential costs resulting from a change in volume; Closing a plant; Differential costs at capacity; Wearing out a production line; Accounting for differential costs; Using an asset already owned. Profit-Volume Analysis: Construction of breakeven and profit-volume charts; Uses of profit-volume and breakeven charts.

10. Two Special Control Techniques   *156*

Control of Purchased Material Costs: Standard costs and material cost control; Situations requiring material cost controls; Purchased material control system—differentiated products; Purchased material control system—common products; Summary. The Standard Selling Price: Developing standard prices; The standard price report; Who should prepare a standard price report?; Advantage of a standard price report. Summary.

11. Evaluating a Control System   *167*

Evaluating an Existing Control System: Analyzing the existing system; Deciding on the changes to be made. Some General Rules for Revising a Control System: 1. The simplest system is the best; 2. Do not forget informal communication; 3. All control systems should be tailor-made; 4. A standard cost system does not automatically mean that costs are controlled; 5. Impractical recommendations are useless; 6. Remember that change is painful; 7. People, not reports, make a control system effective; 8. A control system is not a panacea for poor management; 9. Be realistic about timetables; 10. Plan the system with the future in mind. Summary.

Appendix A. Profit Planning, *by Marshall K. Evans*   *179*

The Profit Pattern. Segregating Costs: Product costs; Committed costs; Managed costs. Graphic Analysis. Understanding the Causes: Interpretation; Changes over time; Analysis form; Basic

Cost and
Budget Analysis

CHAPTER ONE

Cost Accounting Systems

The purpose of this chapter is to describe the general characteristics of each of the basic kinds of cost accounting systems, to demonstrate the elementary accounting mechanics required by each, and, finally, to explain under what conditions each of these systems should be used.

Purposes of a Cost Accounting System

A cost accounting system has three principal purposes:

1. To provide the values of the Work-in-Process and Finished Goods Inventories (this information is required for profit determination);
2. To provide data for cost control; and
3. To provide data for revenue decisions (for example, changing the price, dropping an unprofitable product, or changing the sales mix).

All cost accounting systems are not set up to accomplish all three of these purposes. In many cases, the only use of the cost system is to value inventories. (This is all right if the other two functions are unimportant or are accomplished through other means.) In evaluating any cost system, the following questions should be answered:

1

1. What is the cost accounting system supposed to accomplish? (That is, which of the three principal purposes?)
2. How well does the system do what it is supposed to accomplish?
3. Should it be accomplishing more? (For example, if it does not provide cost control information, should it?)
4. Does the system accomplish what it is supposed to do as efficiently as possible? (For example, if the system is used only for inventory valuation, does it also supply detail unnecessary to this purpose?)

Types of Cost Systems

Cost accounting systems are traditionally divided into job order cost, process cost, and standard cost. In most complex cost accounting systems, however, combinations of all three types will be found. In this chapter, a "pure" type of each system will be described first; a description of two typical combination systems is included at the end of the chapter.

Books of Original Entry

The books of original entry are not treated in this book except through the use of summarized general journal entries. The basic principle is setting up the books of original entry in a cost accounting system (or any accounting system, for that matter) is to minimize the clerical costs, consistent with good internal control. Setting up an efficient clerical system for recording the basic cost accounting facts is largely a specialized problem in data processing. Except in unusual circumstances, it is not necessary for management to be familiar with the methods of collecting the cost accounting data in order to understand the meaning of the data and to use this information as a basis for making decisions.

The Cost Ledger

This chapter is concerned primarily with the flow of information through the ledger. First, the ledger is the key to any cost accounting system, because it determines the information that the system will provide on a regular basis. For example, if there is no account in the ledger where the cost of "scrap" is accumulated, this information cannot be obtained without a special study (and sometimes not even then).

Second, it is always possible to accumulate almost any amount of information outside of the books of account; this is usually referred to as "statistical data" to distinguish it from accounting data. It is important to know what information comes from the books of account and what information is generated outside of the accounting system. Although accounting data may not be more accurate than statistical data, they are collected with the use of consistent and generally rigorous rules. The quality of statistical data is subject to wider variations.

Third, a general understanding of the cost ledger is important to management because it gives them an insight into the kind of information that they should be receiving from their cost accounting system.

SECTION I. JOB ORDER COST ACCOUNTING

A job order cost system has the following characteristics:

1. The production process is set up on the basis of a number of separate assignments or jobs.
2. Each job is assigned a number or some other distinguishing symbol, and a separate accounting document (usually a job order card) is set up for each job.
3. All direct material and direct labor put into process are designated as applying to a specific job and recorded on a job order card.
4. Overhead costs are allocated to each job, usually on the basis of the relative amount of direct labor.
5. The Work-in-Process Inventory value is the sum of the amounts on the incomplete job order cards.

Job Order Card

The job order card may take a variety of forms. One of the simplest is an 8½ by 11-inch card that specifies the job number and job description on the top and has columns for accumulating material, labor and overhead costs on the bottom. An example of such a card follows:

XYZ COMPANY   Job No. _86432_

Description: ___6,000 – 6" Widgets, Chrome-steel alloy___

Date	Material	Dept. A Labor	Dept. B Labor	Dept. A Overhead	Dept. B Overhead	Total
Jan.	$ 62 00	$ 10 00	$ 20 00	$ 20 00	$ 20 00	$ 132 00
Feb.			30 00		30 00	60 00

Direct Material

As material is purchased, the entry in the ledger is to debit Raw Materials Inventory and to credit Accounts Payable. Raw materials are issued on requisitions that identify the specific job on which the material will be used. Periodically, these requisitions are summarized and the amounts applicable to each job are entered on the individual job order cards. The total of the amounts recorded on the job order cards is entered in the general ledger as a debit to Work-in-Process Inventory and a credit to Raw Materials Inventory.

For example, during the month of January, material costing $1,500 has been requisitioned as follows: Job 101, $900; Job 102, $200; Job 103, $400.

The entry is:

Work-in-Process Inventory $1,500
    Raw Materials Inventory $1,500

At the same time, the amount of the material requisitioned for each job is recorded on the appropriate job order cards. (The sum of the material costs on the job order cards will be equal to the value of the raw material in process.)

Direct Labor

Direct labor is handled in the same way as direct material, except, of course, that there is no account to correspond to the Raw Material Inventory. The direct labor payroll is broken down by jobs. Usually this is done by having each man fill out a time card showing how much time was spent on each job. The accounting entry is to debit Work-in-Process Inventory and credit Accrued Wages Payable. At the same time, an entry is made on each job order card to record the direct labor cost applicable to that job.

For example, the following direct labor costs were incurred during the month of January:

Job	Dept. A	Dept. B	Total
101	$30	$40	$ 70
102	60	50	110
103	90	10	100
TOTAL	$180	$100	$280

The entry is:

Work-in-Process Inventory $280
    Accrued Wages Payable $280

The labor cost applicable to each job is also recorded on the appropriate job order card. (The total of the labor on the job order cards is equal to the amount of direct labor in process.)

Overhead

There are two customary ways of handling overhead in a job order cost system: one is to apply all overhead costs incurred during a period to the job worked on during that period; the other is to use a standard overhead rate. The latter method is usually employed for reasons explained below.

Actual Overhead Rate. The first problem is to decide on a method for allocating overhead to specific jobs. The usual method is to allocate overhead in proportion to the relative amount of direct labor (either dollars or hours) employed on each job. Two other methods are (a) the relative amount of direct material; (b) the relative number of machine hours. The principle, of course, is to use the base that most closely assigns overhead costs to the jobs that are responsible for generating these costs. At best, however, a single allocation base will be more or less arbitrary.

Once the basis of allocation has been decided upon, the method of allocating overhead to individual jobs is as follows:

(a) Calculate the total direct labor (or other allocation base) and the total overhead costs incurred during the period. (This is usually done by department.)

(b) Divide the direct labor amount into the overhead amount to obtain the overhead rate. (If done by department, there will be several departmental rates.)

(c) Multiply the overhead rate by the direct labor incurred on each job. (This will also be done by department where there are departmental rates.) This is the overhead applicable to each job.

(d) Debit Work-in-Process Inventory and credit the overhead account for the total amount.

For example:

Direct Labor:

Job 101	$ 70
Job 102	110
Job 103	100
TOTAL	$280

Overhead:

Indirect Labor	$200
Supplies	150
Utilities	250
Depreciation	100
TOTAL	$700

The journal entries are:

(1)

Work-in-Process Inventory $280
    Accrued Wages Payable $280

(Note that these amounts are also entered on the job order cards.)

(2)

Indirect Labor $200
    Accrued Wages Payable $200

(3)

Supplies $150
Utilities 250
    Accounts Payable $400

(4)

Depreciation Expense $100
    Accumulated Depreciation $100

(5)

Overhead Summary $700
    Indirect Labor $200
    Supplies   150
    Utilities   250
    Depreciation   100

(6)

Work-in-Process Inventory $700
    Overhead Summary $700

(Note that the overhead rate is 700/280, or 250%. Therefore, Job 101 is charged with $175; Job 102, with $275; Job 103, with $250.)

Under this system of overhead allocation, there is never any under- or over-absorbed overhead, because the rate is calculated *after* the total direct labor and overhead costs are known. The difficulty with this method is that the overhead rate can fluctuate widely from month to month, depending upon the volume of operations. This can result in significantly different costs for the same item produced in different periods even though efficiency and price levels have remained constant. Pricing action and cost control usually are difficult under such circumstances. Even inventory values may be seriously distorted.

Standard Overhead Rate. Under this method of overhead allocation, a *standard* overhead rate is established at the beginning of the year. This rate is obtained by dividing the estimated direct labor at standard volume (or estimated actual volume) into the total estimated overhead at the same volume. (Standard volume represents a normal long-range level of sales.) The rate is used throughout the year to calculate the burden applicable to each job.

The actual volume of production usually varies from the standard (or forecast) volume and the actual costs usually vary from the estimates. Consequently, the standard overhead rate rarely results in allocating to specific jobs exactly all of the actual overhead costs. The amount by which actual overhead is different from that allocated to the various jobs is called *over-* or *under-absorbed overhead*. This amount is usually written off directly to the Cost of Sales.

For example, all of the facts are the same as in the previous case, except that a standard overhead absorption rate of 200 per cent was used to calculate the overhead applicable to each job. The journal entries are unchanged, except that entry (6) now is

Work-in-Process $560
    Overhead Summary $560

(Note that the overhead rate is 200 per cent; therefore, Job 101 is charged with $140; Job 102, with $220; Job 103; with $200.)

An additional entry is required to close the Overhead Summary account, as follows:

Cost of Sales $140
    Overhead Summary $140

Completed Jobs

When a job is completed, the Finished Goods Inventory is debited and the Work-in-Process Inventory is credited with the cost of the completed job. For example, if the job illustrated on page 3 was completed without further costs, the entry would be:

Finished Goods Inventory $192
    Work-in-Process Inventory $192

Frequently the Work-in-Process Inventory is subdivided by cost element and department. If this was the case, the entry would be:

Finished Goods Inventory $192
    Work-in-Process Inventory—Material $62
    Work-in-Process Inventory—Dept. A Labor 10
    Work-in-Process Inventory—Dept. B Labor 50
    Work-in-Process Inventory—Dept. A Overhead 20
    Work-in-Process Inventory—Dept. B Overhead 50

Uses of Job Order Costing

A job order system of cost accounting is commonly used when two conditions exist: (1) when there is a large number of different jobs, and (2) when management needs to know the cost of each job. An illustration of this is a contract calling for a price determined by the cost plus a fixed fee. In other cases where the price is fixed beforehand by means of a bid, management will need to know the actual costs so that they can be compared with the estimate used to determine the bid. This information may be useful in determining the accuracy of the cost estimate or the efficiency of the cost performance. A job order system will also provide management with profits by jobs. Such a breakdown of profits may be useful in deciding what kind of job should be undertaken.

SECTION II. PROCESS COST ACCOUNTING

A process cost accounting system is best adapted to an operation in which all products produced in a particular department are identical. (A condition diametric to that found in the usual job order system, which is best adapted to an operation in which all jobs are different.)

The characteristics of a process cost accounting system are:

(1) Costs are accumulated by department or cost center.
(2) The costs of the service departments are allocated to the productive departments so that all costs are eventually charged to some productive department. (This is also true of a job order system that develops departmental overhead rates.)
(3) The number of units produced in each productive department is calculated.
(4) The number of units produced in each productive department is divided into the total cost assigned to the department; this is the cost per unit for that department. The total cost of the finished product is obtained by summing the unit costs of all of the departments through which the product passed.

Direct Departmental Costs

Under a process cost system, costs are charged directly to the department that incurs them to the extent that this is possible. For example, material is requisitioned and charged to the department that uses it; direct labor costs are charged to the productive department employing the direct labor. Wages of indirect employees (such as foremen, inspectors, or material handlers) are charged to the department for which they work; as supplies are requisitioned, a record is kept of the department to which they are sent; depreciation of equipment is charged to the department that uses the equipment.

Departments are either productive or service. A productive department is one that contributes directly to the production of the product being manufactured. A service department does not contribute directly to production but, rather, provides a service to the productive departments. Examples of service departments are maintenance, plant accounting, industrial relations, and quality control. In addition to service departments, there are also certain cost centers that accumulate costs applicable to the entire plant, for example, building depreciation and maintenance.

Usually, the department expense account is divided into several subaccounts. For example, there could be the following accounts in Department A:

Department A—Direct Material
Department A—Direct Labor
Department A—Indirect Labor
Department A—Supplies
Department A—Utilities
Department A—Depreciation

The number and type of subaccounts depend upon how much departmental cost information is desired. Some companies use more than a hundred subaccounts for each department.

The entries to record direct departmental costs are quite simple. For material, it is a debit to Department A—Direct Material and a credit to Raw Materials Inventory; for direct labor, it is a debit to Department A—Direct Labor and a credit to Accrued Wages Payable. Overhead expenses are handled in the same manner: the debit is to Department A (the particular overhead account to be recorded) and the credit is to Cash, Accounts Payable, and so forth.

Allocation of Service Department Expense

Since all product costs in a process cost accounting system must be charged to some productive department, service activities (such as quality control or maintenance) and over-all plant cost centers (such as building depreciation or plant manager's office) must be allocated to the productive departments. The simplest way of doing this is to accumulate the total direct costs for each of the service activities and then to allocate these costs to productive departments based on the best measure of the relative service performed. Some usual bases for allocation are:

Direct labor dollars for the plant manager's office;
Floor space for building depreciation, heat, janitor service, building repairs, rent;
Number of people for the industrial relations department.
Some service departments (such as Maintenance) may keep records

of the service provided to each productive department and allocate costs on this basis.

In a plant having three productive departments—A, B, and C—and two indirect expense categories—plant superintendence and building depreciation—the direct labor costs and floor space for the productive departments are as follows:

Department	Direct Labor	Floor Space
A	$ 6,000	2,500 sq. ft.
B	10,000	2,500
C	4,000	5,000
TOTAL	$20,000	10,000 sq. ft.

If the cost of plant superintendence is $6,000 and building depreciation is $20,000, the allocations would be as follows:

Department	Superintendence		Building Maintenance	
	Amount	Per Cent	Amount	Per Cent
A	$1,800	30%	$5,000	25%
B	3,000	50	5,000	25
C	1,200	20	10,000	50
TOTAL	$6,000	100%	$20,000	100%

The accounting entries for recording charges to service departments are exactly the same as the entries for charging costs to productive departments. At the end of each month, however, the service departments are credited and the productive departments are debited for the amount accumulated in the service department accounts. In the case of plant superintendence above, the entries would be:

Department A—Superintendence	$1,800	
Department B—Superintendence	3,000	
Department C—Superintendence	1,200	
Superintendence—Allocations Out		$6,000

The method just described for allocating costs to productive departments is perhaps the simplest approach to the problem. In general, the simpler methods of allocation are the most satisfactory because, at best, most allocations are quite arbitrary. Occasionally, however, more complicated methods of allocation are justified. These methods are described in Chapter 3.

Number of Units Produced

After all costs have been assigned to some productive department, it is necessary to know the number of units produced by each department in order to calculate the cost per unit. The main problem is to determine the Work-in-Process Inventory in equivalent units. (Two half-completed units are equal to one completed unit.) Sometimes, when direct materials are put into process at the beginning of the production cycle, it is useful to separate material costs from other costs. For example, the Work-in-Process Inventory might include 100 per cent of the materials required for completion but have only 50 per cent of the required direct labor and overhead.

In calculating the Work-in-Process Inventory, an estimate must be made of both the number of units in the process of being produced and the per cent of completion. This provides the basis for translating the Work-in-Process Inventory into equivalent finished units. The formula for computing the number of equivalent units produced during a period is this: ending Work-in-Process Inventory in equivalent units plus the number of units completed and transferred out of the department minus the beginning Work-in-Process Inventory in equivalent units.

Valuation of Work-in-Process Inventory

The units produced divided into the departmental costs provide the cost per unit for the department. The value of the Work-in-Process Inventory is calculated by multiplying the total cost per unit by the number of equivalent units. When more than one department is involved in making a product, the cost of all the other departments must also be included. The value transferred to the Finished Goods Inventory account is calculated by adding the beginning Work-in-Process Inventory to the total costs incurred during the period and subtracting the value of the ending Work-in-Process Inventory.

A Process Cost Problem

The D. French Company has three producing departments, A, B, and C, and two service departments, Y and Z. It makes two products: Product 1 and Product 2. Both products enter Department A but Product 1 is completed by Department B and Product 2 is completed by Department C. The costs incurred during the month were:

Department A $40,000
Department B 20,000

Department C 20,000
Department Y 6,000
Department Z 4,000

The Work-in-Process Inventory and the production statistics were as follows:

	Department A	Department B	Department C
Beginning Work-in-Process Inventory:			
Units	5,000	3,000	4,000
% Completion	50%	25%	30%
Value of Beginning Work-in-Process			
Inventory	$12,500	$17,625	$29,600
Units Completed During Month	10,000	6,000	3,000
Ending Work-in-Process Inventory:			
Units	4,000	4,000	4,000
% Completion	50%	30%	25%

The costs of service departments Y and Z are allocated to the production departments on the basis of their relative direct costs.

Solution. The entries to record the basic expenses would be a debit to the department and subclassification (for example, Department A— Material, Department B—Utilities) and a credit to Accounts Payable, cash, and so forth.

After recording all expenses in some department or cost center, the next step is to allocate all costs to productive departments. In this case the distribution of expenses of Departments Y and Z is as follows:

	Amount	Per Cent
Department A	$5,000	50%
Department B	2,500	25
Department C	2,500	25
	$10,000	100%

The entry is:

Department A $5,000
Department B 2,500
Department C 2,500
    Department Y $6,000
    Department Z   4,000

After all expenses have been allocated to the productive departments, the value of the ending Work-in-Process Inventory is calculated.

The first step is to compute the number of units produced and the cost per unit. This is done as follows:

	Department A	Department B	Department C
Ending Inventory (Equivalent Units)	2,000	1,200	1,000
Production Completed During Period	10,000	6,000	3,000
TOTAL	12,000	7,000	4,000
Less Beginning Inventory (Equivalent Units) ..	2,500	750	1,200
Units Produced	9,500	6,450	2,800
Total Cost of Production	$45,000	$22,500	$22,500
Cost per Unit	4.76	3.50	8.40

The value of the ending Work-in-Process Inventory is calculated as follows:

$$
\begin{array}{rll}
\text{Department A} = 2,000 & \times\ 4.76\ = & \$\ 9,520 \\
\text{Department B} = 4,000^* & \times\ 4.76\ = & 19,040 \\
1,200 & \times\ 3.50\ = & 4,200 \\
\end{array}
$$

$$
\begin{array}{rll}
\text{TOTAL} & & \$23,240 \\
\text{Department C} = 4,000^* & \times\ 4.76\ = & \$19,040 \\
= 1,000 & \times\ 8.04\ = & 8,040 \\
\end{array}
$$

$$
\begin{array}{ll}
\text{TOTAL} & \$27,080 \\
\end{array}
$$

Total Work-in-Process Inventory $59,840

* These units have been completed by Department A and transferred to Departments B and C. They are, therefore, 100 per cent completed with respect to the cost incurred in Department A.

The entry transferring values from Work-in-Process to Finished Goods is calculated as follows:

	Department A	Department B	Department C
Beginning Inventory	$12,500	$17,625	$29,600
Cost Incurred	45,000	22,500	22,500
TOTAL	$57,500	$40,125	$52,100
Less Ending Inventory	9,520	23,240	27,080
Value of Goods Transferred to Finished Goods Inventory	$47,980	$16,885	$25,020

The entries are:

Department B	$33,586	
Department C	$14,394	
Department A		$47,980

(Department A completed and transferred 10,000 units. Of these 7,000 went to B and 3,000 went to C. [Six thousand units completed plus 4,000 units in the ending inventory minus 3,000 in the beginning inventory means that 7,000 were received into Department B. The same kind of analysis shows that 3,000 were received in Department C.] Accordingly, B gets $7/10$ of the value of goods transferred and C gets $3/10$ of the value.)

The final entry is:

Finished Goods	$89,885	
Department B		$50,471
Department C		$39,414

Uses of a Process Cost Accounting System

Pure process cost accounting systems, similar to that described above, have limited usefulness. Most complex manufacturing operations cannot use a process cost system because this system can only be used when each department or cost center produces an identical (or nearly identical) product. The type of production most suitable to a process cost accounting system is also most suited to a standard cost system. As explained in the next section, a standard cost system will usually provide better management information than an actual cost system. In general, therefore, most process cost systems would be better changed to a standard cost system. This may not be true in every case, but there should be a good reason why a process cost system is *necessary* and why a standard cost system is *not*.

SECTION III. STANDARD COSTS

The two methods of cost accounting described in the preceding sections are known as "historical" cost methods because they are designed to provide estimates of "actual" costs. The objective of the historical cost accounting system is to determine the amounts spent in producing the products, and to use these amounts to calculate the unit costs and, subsequently, the inventory values.

A standard cost system differs from an historical cost system in that it *starts* with the unit cost. The standard unit cost, instead of being calculated from historical cost data, is determined by estimating the amount that the product "should" cost; these cost estimates are made on the basis of the material specifications and production processes. The standard cost represents a "normal" or, sometimes, an "objective" cost.

A standard cost system cannot be differentiated from a job order or process cost system; cost standards can be used in conjunction with both job order and process costing. The distinction is between an historical and a standard cost system although, even here, a cost accounting system can be a combination of historical and standard costing. (For example, material costs can be historical and labor and overhead can be standard.) The distinguishing characteristic of the standard cost system is that it starts with a unit cost that has been developed analytically and it does not normally provide the "actual" unit cost incurred during a given period; Work-in-Process and Finished Goods Inventories are valued at standard cost.

There are two principal types of standard cost systems: *Actual-in, Standard-out,* and *Standard-in, Standard-out.*

Actual-in, Standard-out

The term "actual-in, standard-out" refers to the Work-in-Process Inventory. When this method is used, actual costs are debited to the Work-in-Process Inventory account as they are incurred during the production process; when products have been completed, the Work-in-Process Inventory account is credited for the *standard* cost of the completed products. Specifically, the method operates as follows:

1. During the month the expense accounts are debited as incurred. For example, Direct Material will be debited and Raw Materials Inventory credited for the value of the direct material requisitioned; Direct Labor and Indirect Labor are debited and Accrued Wages Payable is credited for the weekly payroll; Utility Expense is debited and Accounts Payable is credited for the cost of the utilities used during the month. (Note: these expenses will usually be classified by department. This explanation assumes a one-department plant for simplicity.)
2. At the end of the month, adjusting entries are recorded to bring all costs up to date. For example, Depreciation Expense is debited and Accumulated Depreciation is credited for the monthly depreciation cost.
3. The actual costs are next closed to the Work-in-Process Inventory account.[1] For example, the expense accounts are as follows: Raw Materials, $15,000; Direct Labor, $10,000; Indirect Labor, $8,000; Utilities, $3,000; and Depreciation, $2,000. The accounting entries are:

Overhead Summary	$13,000	
Indirect Labor		$8,000
Utilities		3,000
Depreciation		2,000
Work-in-Process Inventory	$38,000	
Material		$15,000
Direct Labor		10,000
Overhead Summary		13,000

[1] A common method is to include all manufacturing expense accounts as subdivisions of the Work-in-Process Inventory account. If this has been done, the entry to Work-in-Process is unnecessary, All other entries would be the same.

4. The Finished Goods Inventory is debited and Work-in-Process Inventory is credited with the standard cost of all the goods completed and transferred.

5. The value of the Work-in-Process Inventory at the end of the month is estimated by taking a physical inventory of partially completed units, converting these to equivalent completed units, and multiplying the number of units by the standard cost per unit. The difference between this amount and the balance in the Work-in-Process Inventory account is principally the result of differences between actual and standard costs. (Under some conditions, spoilage and pilferage could account for part of the difference.) The Work-in-Process Inventory account is then adjusted to its standard cost value by crediting Work-in-Process Inventory and debiting a variance account for the difference between the actual balance in the Work-in-Process Inventory account and the standard cost value of the physical inventory. (The reverse entry would be made if the physical inventory at standard cost showed a value greater than that reflected in the Work-in-Process Inventory account.)

6. The variance account is closed to the Cost of Sales account.

Under the method just described, there is only a single variance account. By subdividing the Work-in-Process account into material, labor, and overhead the variance by cost category may be obtained. In practice, the Work-in-Process account is usually subdivided by department as well; in this way, the variance from standard is available by type of cost and by department.

The main disadvantage of the actual-in, standard-out method of standard cost accounting is that a physical inventory must be taken each month.

Standard-in, Standard-out

As the name implies, the standard-in, standard-out method is one in which the Work-in-Process Inventory account is debited with the standard costs of the products worked upon during the period and credited with the standard costs of the goods completed and transferred to finished goods.

Specifically, the standard-in, standard-out method operates as follows:

1. The entries to the basic expense accounts are the same as described in items 1 and 2 under the actual-in, standard-out method.

2. The individual overhead cost accounts are usually closed to a summary account in the same way as under item 3 of the actual-in, standard-out method.

3. The Material, Labor, and Overhead Summary accounts are credited with the *standard cost* of the items produced during the period. The amount left in these accounts is the variance: favorable if the balance is a credit; unfavorable if the balance is a debit. In order to make this calculation, it is necessary to know the number of units produced. This is no problem if there is no beginning and ending Work-in-Process Inventory or if the beginning and ending Work-in-Process Inventory is the same. If the beginning and ending Work-in-Process Inventory is significant and different, however, it is necessary to estimate the equivalent units produced. This is done in the same manner as described in the section on process cost accounting. (If the Work-in-Process Inventory does not vary much from month to month, it can be ignored, and the number of units completed can be used to approximate the number of units produced.)

4. The balances in the Material, Labor, and Overhead Summary accounts are closed to a variance account; this, in turn, is closed to the Cost of Sales account.

5. The final entry is to debit the Finished Goods Inventory and credit the Work-in-Process Inventory for the standard cost of the units completed during the period.

The standard-in, standard-out method has the advantage of not requiring a monthly physical inventory. There is always the possibility, however, of overstating the value of the Work-in-Process Inventory. If scrap is not carefully controlled, the actual value of the inventory will be smaller than the amount shown in the Work-in-Process account. The inventory is credited only for the units that have been completed; if units are scrapped or stolen, the value remains on the books until a physical inventory is taken.

Uses of Standard Costs

A standard cost system is usually superior to an historical cost system for most management purposes. First, standard costs provide a better base for revenue decisions than historical costs do. Standard costs are calculated at a normal volume and represent a reasonable degree of efficiency. Random fluctuations in volume and cost levels, which cause wide fluctuations in historical costs, are not present in standard costs.

Second, standard costs are a more effective cost control tool than most historical costs because they provide a comparison of actual costs with predetermined standards. (Although, as will be shown in later chapters, standard costs are not as effective a cost control tool as many accountants appear to believe.)

Third, the clerical costs required to maintain a standard cost system are less than those required in most historical cost systems. In fact, in a complex production process, some form of standard costing is the only practical method. (It should be noted, however, that the cost of establishing and maintaining standards will tend to offset this advantage.)

A standard cost system can be used under nearly any productive system and is generally preferred to an historical cost system. A standard cost system would normally not be used, however, when each job is different or when it is important to know the historical cost (as in certain government contracts).

SECTION IV. CALCULATING ACTUAL UNIT COSTS IN COMPLEX MANUFACTURING PROCESSES

The manufacturing processes of many companies are such that neither a pure job cost system nor a pure process cost system is practical, for example, a company that makes many different kinds of parts but produces a considerable number of each kind. It is not uncommon to have a plant that produces several hundred different parts in quantities of 1,000 to 10,000. Because these are not special order parts, job order costing is not usually appropriate. On the other hand, if there are many parts produced in the same department (and there usually are), process cost accounting is not practical.

In these situations a standard cost system will usually solve the problem. If, however, management wants "actual" costs, a combination system can be developed to provide this information. There are two methods that are most often used to get so-called actual costs: modified job cost and modified standard cost.

Modified Job Cost

If the parts are produced in batches, the easiest way to calculate actual cost is to set up a job order card for each batch and to record the cost of material and direct labor applicable to each batch. When the batch is completed, overhead is assigned (usually on the basis of Direct Labor) and the total cost is divided by the number of units completed to get the cost per unit.

Modified Standard Cost System

Where goods are not produced in batches or where standard costs are available, actual costs can be calculated by using a modified standard cost system. In its simplest form, standard cost variances are allocated to each of the products in proportion to the amount of the standard cost. For example, during the month of January a plant had the following relationship of standard and actual costs:

	Standard	Actual	Actual Under/ (Over) Standard Amount	Per Cent
Material	$50,000	$55,000	($5,000)	(10)%
Direct Labor	15,000	12,000	3,000	20
Overhead	40,000	42,000	(2,000)	(5)

The "actual" cost of each part produced would be the standard cost adjusted for the per cent of variance. For example:

	Part A		
	Standard Cost	Adjustment	Actual Cost
Direct Material	$10.00	+10%	$11.00
Direct Labor	5.00	—20%	4.00
Overhead	10.00	+ 5%	10.50
TOTAL	$25.00		$25.50

A frequent variation of this method is to calculate Direct Labor in this manner and to allocate burden to product based on the labor. (Actual material costs would be calculated in some other way.) For example, if the following costs for a particular month were

Actual Labor	$11,000
Standard Labor	10,000
Actual Burden	22,000

the labor and overhead for Part A would be calculated as follows:

Standard Labor Per Unit	$5.00
Adjustment to Actual	+10%
Actual Direct Labor	$5.50
Actual Overhead Rate	
(22,000 ÷ 11,000)	200%
Actual Overhead	$11.00

WHICH COST ACCOUNTING SYSTEM TO USE?

One of the most persistent fallacies to which many an accountant or manager clings is that actual costs are more accurate than standard costs. This misconception evidently stems from the belief that actual costs are derived from the books of account (whose integrity cannot be questioned) while standard costs are merely the estimates of some cost accountant or industrial engineer. In most complex manufacturing situations, the so-called actual cost is as much an estimate as the standard cost. As demonstrated in the previous section, a standard cost is frequently necessary for calculating an actual cost. A difference between a standard cost system and an actual cost system is that the latter usually provides for all of the costs incurred during a stated period to be applied to some product. This could be a great disadvantage, however, because costs calculated in this manner are frequently subject to such wide fluctuations (changes in volume, for example, can have a significant effect on unit costs). These random fluctuations may make actual costs nearly useless for revenue decisions or evaluating cost performance. The important consideration determining the type of cost accounting system that should be employed is the use to which the figures generated by the system are to be put. To the extent that the system provides estimates of "actual" unit costs, it should be ascertained that these are the figures that management needs to guide it in making correct operating decisions.

SUMMARY

There are three types of "pure" cost accounting systems: job order, process, and standard. The first two are called "historical" cost systems because they assign the costs actually incurred during a period to the products produced during that period. The standard cost system, on the other hand, begins with a unit cost developed analytically. The standard cost per unit multiplied by the number of units produced is compared to the actual costs incurred. The difference between the two figures is called a "variance" and is written off to Cost of Sales each period. In business, most cost accounting systems are combinations of these three types.

In deciding which type of system to use, the question to be answered is: What information does management need? The correct cost accounting system is the one that best provides this information.

In most complex production processes, a standard cost system will be superior to an historical cost system. In cases where an historical cost system is used, there should be positive reasons why this system is superior to a standard cost system.

CHAPTER TWO

Variance Analysis

A variance may be defined as the difference between actual and standard cost. The process of analyzing variances involves subdividing the total variance in such a way that management can assign responsibility for off-standard performance. The analysis of variance among companies ranges from very simple to very complex, depending on such factors as the manufacturing processes, the nature of the standard cost system, the disposition of management, or the degree of sophistication of the controller or chief cost accountant. Some systems provide only for a single total variance amount; others may analyze variances by a dozen different causes. The decision on how far to go in analyzing variances should be based on the use that management has for the information. The analysis of variance should be extended as long as the figures are useful to management in making decisions. The analysis should stop at the point where further breakdown of the variance provides no *useful* additional information to management.

The description of variance analysis has been divided into two parts: simple and complex. This segregation is completely arbitrary; its only purpose is to make the explanation of variance techniques easier to understand.

SIMPLE VARIANCE ANALYSIS

In cases where the beginning Work-in-Process Inventory does not differ significantly from the ending Work-in-Process Inventory, the variance analysis techniques described in this section can be used. Where the beginning and ending Work-in-Process Inventory differs, however, the analysis of variance is more complex and can only be solved by using the methods described in the second part of the chapter.

Variance Matrix

The first step in variance analysis is to break down the total variance by type of cost (Material, Direct Labor, and Overhead). This can be accomplished most easily by setting up a variance matrix, as follows;

	Costs		
	Actual	Absorbed	Budget
Material			
Direct Labor			
Overhead			
TOTAL			

The *actual* costs are, of course, the amount of cost incurred during the period and come directly from the books of account.

The *absorbed* costs are the standard cost per unit multiplied by the number of units produced during the period. In many standard cost systems, these figures are also available from the books of account.

The *budgeted* costs are the same as the absorbed costs except for the overhead amount. The budgeted overhead is obtained from the flexible budget equation. A detailed description of flexible budgeting is included in Chapter 6. For the purpose of this chapter, it is sufficient to understand that the overhead budget includes a fixed element (for example, depreciation) that will not vary with the volume of production and a variable element (for example, supplies) that will. The budget equation divides the standard cost into its fixed and variable elements to indicate how much overhead cost *should* have been incurred during a particular month. This equation is as follows:

$y = a + bx$, where
$y =$ the amount of budgeted overhead at volume x;
$a =$ total standard fixed costs per month;
$b =$ standard variable cost per unit of production;
$x =$ number of units produced during the month.

The budget authorization is required to separate the volume variance (the responsibility of the sales department) from the spending variance (the responsibility of the plant manager). If the control system does not employ a flexible budget, the spending variance cannot be separated. (In this case, the overhead variance does not indicate the efficiency of the operations.)

The following equations are used to analyze the variances: (notice that a negative value is an unfavorable variance and a positive value is a favorable variance):

$$\text{Material Variance} = \text{ABSORBED} - \text{Actual}$$
$$\text{Labor Variance} = \text{ABSORBED} - \text{Actual}$$

Overhead Variances:

$$\text{Spending} = \text{BUDGET} - \text{Actual}$$
$$\text{Volume} = \text{ABSORBED} - \text{Budget}$$

For example:

	Actual Costs	Standard Costs	Budgeted Costs
Material	$27,000	$3.00 per unit	$3.00 per unit
Labor	8,000	1.00 per unit	1.00 per unit
Overhead	20,000	2.00 per unit	(10,000 fixed + $1.00 per unit variable)

Standard Volume = 10,000 units; Actual Volume = 9,000 units.

The variance matrix is as follows:

	Actual	Absorbed	Budget
Material	$27,000	$27,000	$27,000
Labor	8,000	9,000	9,000
Overhead	20,000	18,000	19,000
TOTAL	$55,000	$54,000	$55,000

Variance Analysis:
Material Variance = 27,000 − 27,000 = 0
Labor Variance = 9,000 − 8,000 = 1,000 favorable
Overhead-Spending = 19,000 − 20,000 = 1,000 unfavorable
Overhead-Volume = 18,000 − 19,000 = 1,000 unfavorable
Net Variance = 1,000 unfavorable

Analysis by Cause

The next step is to break down the variances by cause so that management will know what action, if any, is required.

MATERIAL

The material variance is usually separated into price and usage. Price variance results from paying a price that is higher than standard for the material; this is normally the responsibility of the purchasing department. Usage variance results from using more than the standard quantity; this is normally the responsibility of the plant manager. The equations for calculating these variances follow. (In these equations, also, a negative value is an unfavorable variance and a positive value is favorable.)

Price Variance = Actual usage at standard prices minus
. actual usage at actual prices.
Usage Variance = Total material variance minus price variance.

or

Usage Variance = Standard usage at actual prices minus actual
usage at actual prices.
Price Variance = Total material variance minus usage variance.

Because the two types of variance are interrelated, the second variance is calculated by subtracting the first type from the total. Otherwise, the sum of the two variances will be different from the total variance. It makes no difference which one is calculated first. These variances are only approximations and the fact that the amounts will differ (depending on the method of calculation) is not important. The general rule (but by no means absolute) is to calculate the most controllable variance first. For example, if it was decided that price variance was the most controllable, the first method described above is used; if usage was the most controllable, the second method is preferred.

DIRECT LABOR

Labor variance is usually separated into rate variance and efficiency variance. The former results from paying the direct labor at a rate higher than standard; the latter results from using more than the standard number of hours.

The equations for calculating the labor variances are as follows:

Efficiency Variance = Standard hours at actual rates minus actual hours
at actual rates.
Rate Variance = Total labor variance minus efficiency variance.

or

Rate Variance = Actual hours at standard rate minus actual hours at ac-
tual rate.
Efficiency Variance = Total labor variance minus rate variance.
(The same interrelationship that exists in the material variances also occurs in the labor variances.)

OVERHEAD

The *spending variance* is sometimes broken down into efficiency variance and price variance. When done, the calculation is the same as that used in the material and labor variance analysis. A much more useful breakdown of overhead spending variance, however, is by account series. Chapter 6 includes a description of the flexible budget performance report, which provides such an analysis. The *volume variance* is not subdivided further.

The overhead variance has already been separated into volume and spending by the variance matrix.

SUMMARY

Type of Variance	*Responsibility*
Material Price Variance	Purchasing Department
Material Usage Variance	Plant Manager
Labor Efficiency Variance	Plant Manager
Rate Variance	Industrial Relations Department or Plant Manager (when a man works out of his classification)
Overhead Volume Variance	Sales Department
Overhead Spending Variance	Plant Manager

COMPLEX VARIANCE ANALYSIS

This section of the chapter describes techniques for solving variance analysis problems of a more complex nature than those just described. These problems occur when the beginning and ending Work-in-Process Inventory is significantly different or when the variance must be broken down into more than two categories for any type of cost.

Material Variance

The most complex variance analysis occurs with respect to material. In the previous section, the material variance was obtained by subtracting the actual cost of the material used from the standard cost. Because the beginning and ending Work-in-Process Inventory was equal, the actual cost of the material used was equal to the cost of the material put into production. The standard cost of the material used was calculated by multiplying the number of completed units by the standard cost per unit. This calculation becomes considerably more complex, however, when the beginning Work-in-Process Inventory differs from the ending. In this case, it is necessary to determine the equivalent production in order to calculate the actual and standard cost of the material used. The problem becomes even more complex when the mix of raw materials varies. The following example demonstrates the technique for analyzing material variances in such a complex situation.

Example—The Birmingham Chemical Works

The Birmingham Chemical Works manufactures commercial tile. One of its largest volume items, Microfer, consists of four types of material: A, B, C, and D. A standard cost card (Exhibit 1) shows the standard quantities for a typical batch. In mixing a batch of material for the production of Microfer, it was often necessary to alter the standard proportions of materials used in order to get a mixture of the desired quality and consistency.

At the end of January, the information with respect to Microfer production was as follows:

Exhibit 1
Standard Cost Sheet
MICROFER

Type of Raw Material	Quantity Amount	% of Total	Standard Price Per Pound	Standard Material Cost
A	100 pounds	10%	$.10	$10.00
B	400	40	.05	20.00
C	400	40	.01	4.00
D	100	10	.26	26.00
TOTAL	1,000 pounds	100%		$60.00

$$\text{Standard Cost Per Pound} = \frac{\$60.00}{1,000} = \$.06$$

Standard Usage = 200 pounds per 100 square feet of tile
Standard Cost Per 100 Square Feet = 200 × .06 = $12.00

Exhibit 2
Materials Purchased During the Month

A	40,000 pounds at 11.0¢ per pound =	$ 4,400
B	80,000 pounds at 6.0¢ per pound =	4,800
C	80,000 pounds at 1.0¢ per pound =	800
D	4,000 pounds at 22.5¢ per pound =	900
	182,000 pounds	$10,900

Exhibit 3
Quantities of Material Put into Process During the Month

A	60,000 pounds
B	250,000 pounds
C	200,000 pounds
D	5,000 pounds
TOTAL	515,000 pounds

Exhibit 4

Work-in-Process Inventory and Production

Beginning inventory-in-process .... 15,000 pounds
Ending inventory-in-process .... 30,000 pounds
Production during month .... 245,000 square feet of tile

(The company made the assumption that the inventory at the close of any period contained the standard mix of materials.)

Price Variance

The price variance is calculated as follows:

Amount Purchased	Actual Price	Standard Price	Variance Favorable/(Unfavorable)	
			Unit	Total
40,000	$.110	$.100	$(.010)	$(400)
80,000	.060	.050	(.010)	(800)
80,000	.010	.010	—	—
4,000	.225	.260	.035	140
		TOTAL		$(1,060)

Notice that the material price variance is calculated on the basis of material *purchased*. This method is used when materials are recorded into the Raw Materials Inventory account at the standard price. Any variance from standard is written off, therefore, in the period when the goods are *purchased*. If material is included in the Raw Materials Inventory account at actual cost and transferred to Work-in-Process at standard cost, the price variance will be recorded in the period that the material was *put into process*. In this case, the actual cost of the material put into process was not given and, consequently, it is not possible to calculate the price variance on the basis of the material put into production.

Mix and Usage Variance

The two variances left to be calculated are mix and usage. There is still the problem, described in the first part of the chapter, of the interrelationship of the variances. Where the total variance is separated into only two causes, the problem can be avoided by subtracting the first variance to be calculated from the total variance. Where the variance is separated into more than two causes, it is necessary to use a different method. After calculating the first type of variance (for example, price), use standard prices in all subsequent calculations. After calculating the second type of variance (for example, usage), use the standard price and standard usage in subsequent calculations. In the above example, once having calculated price variance, all subsequent calculations should use standard prices. Then, after the mix variance is calculated, the usage variance should be calculated using *standard price and mix.*

The following steps are required to calculate the total material variance (exclusive of the price variance which has already been isolated):

1. Calculate the cost of material used by multiplying the actual pounds of material used in the finished production (at actual mix) by the standard prices.
2. Calculate the standard cost of material used by multiplying the standard quantity of material in the finished production by the standard price per pound at the standard mix.
3. Subtract the actual from the standard; this is the total mix and usage variance.

ACTUAL COST OF MATERIAL

The actual quantities of material used are calculated as follows:

Type of Material	Beginning Inventory [a]	Quantities Put in Production	Total	Ending Inventory [a]	Quantity Used
A	1,500	60,000	61,500	3,000	58,500
B	6,000	250,000	256,000	12,000	244,000
C	6,000	200,000	206,000	12,000	194,000
D	1,500	5,000	6,500	3,000	3,500
TOTAL	15,000	515,000	530,000	30,000	500,000

[a] The Work-in-Process Inventory is assumed to be at standard mix. The amounts of each type of material are calculated by applying the standard mix percentages to the total number of pounds in inventory.

The cost of actual material used is calculated as follows:

Type of Material	Quantity Used	Standard Price	Cost
A	58,500	.10	$5,850
B	244,000	.05	12,200
C	194,000	.01	1,940
D	2,500	.26	910
TOTAL	500,000		$20,900

Actual Cost of Material Used = $20,900

Standard Cost of Material Used = 245,000 square feet
        × 2 square feet to the pound × $.06 per pound = $29,400.
Mix and Usage Variance = $29,400 — $20,900 = $8,500 favorable.

In this case it was assumed that the Work-in-Process Inventories were at standard mix and usage. All variances, therefore, must be in the goods that have been completed. For this reason, the actual and standard cost of material in the completed units were calculated. In some cases, however, the ending Work-in-Process Inventory may not be at standard. Under these circumstances, it is necessary to calculate the actual and standard costs of the units produced. The units produced include the equivalent units in the ending inventory as well as the units completed.

MIX VARIANCE

Here procedure for calculating mix variances is as follows:
1. List the actual quantities for each type of material used.
2. List the standard mix for the actual quantities used. (This is done by applying the standard mix percentages for each type of material to the total actual quantity used.)
3. Determine the amount that each type of material varies from the standard.
4. Multiply each of the variances by the standard cost of the material.
5. Add the resulting amounts algebraically; this is the mix variance.

In this procedure, the mix variance is calculated after the price variance but before the usage variance. Therefore, the prices are standard and the quantities used are actual. If the mix variance were calculated after the usage variance, standard quantities would be used.

Calculation of Mix Variance

Type of Material	Actual Quantity at Actual Mix	Actual Quantity at Standard Mix [a]	Variance	Standard Price	Total Variance Favorable/ Unfavorable
A	58,500	50,000	(8,500)	$.10	$(850)
B	244,000	200,000	(44,000)	.05	(2,200)
C	194,000	200,000	6,000	.01	60
D	3,500	50,000	46,500	.26	12,090
TOTAL	500,000	500,000			$ 9,100

[a] Calculated by multiplying the standard mix percentages by the actual number of pounds used.

USAGE VARIANCE

Usage variance can be calculated by subtracting the mix variance from the total variance (total variance [$8,500 favorable] less mix variance [$9,100 favorable] = usage variance, $600 unfavorable) or as follows:

Usage variance = standard quantities in finished production minus actual quantities in finished production multiplied by the standard price per pound at standard mix. This is $[(245,000 \times 2) - 500,000] .06 = 10,000 \times .06 = -\$600$ or $600 unfavorable.

SUMMARY OF MATERIAL VARIANCES

Price	$1,060	Unfavorable
Mix	9,100	Favorable
Usage	600	Unfavorable
NET	$7,440	Favorable

Direct Labor Variance

The calculation of direct labor variances, even when the beginning and ending Work-in-Process Inventories differ, is much simpler than the calculation of material variances. The main problem is to calculate the equivalent number of units produced. The equivalent number of units produced are multiplied by the standard cost per unit to obtain the standard labor cost of the monthly production. The actual labor costs are subtracted to obtain the total labor variance. The total variance is broken down between rate and efficiency by the method described in the first part of the chapter. (There is no problem in obtaining the actual labor costs; this is simply the amount recorded in the Direct Labor Expense account.)

The equation for obtaining equivalent production is as follows: (Ending inventory in equivalent units) + units completed — (Beginning inventory in equivalent units) = equivalent production. (This is the same equation described in Chapter 1 for obtaining units produced in a process cost accounting system.) For example: the standard direct labor cost for each unit of Product A is $1.50; the beginning inventory is 1,000 units, one-half completed; and the ending inventory is 1,800 units, one-third completed. Units completed and transferred to the finished goods inventory equal 5,000. The standard cost of labor = (600 + 5,000 — 500) ($1.50) = $7,650. The actual direct labor cost recorded on the books is subtracted from this amount to obtain the total variance. With additional information, these costs can be broken down into rate and efficiency variance.

Overhead Variance

The method for calculating total overhead variance, in situations where the beginning and ending Work-in-Process Inventory differs, is the same as that described for direct labor. The only complication is to find equivalent units produced and to multiply this number by the standard overhead cost per unit to obtain the total standard overhead cost. Even this complication frequently disappears, however, because the equivalent units produced will already have been calculated in connection with analyzing direct labor variances.

Efficiency Variance

Sometimes the overhead variance is divided into three types: volume, spending, and *efficiency*. An example of this analysis is as follows:

Operating and accounting figures for the month of January with respect to overhead are:

Actual Overhead Cost $8,600
Actual Direct Labor Hours 6,000
Standard Labor Hours 5,500
Budget Equation = $3,000 + $.90 × actual direct labor hours
Absorption Equation = $1.50 × standard direct labor hours

From this information, the following can be calculated:

Absorbed Overhead = 5,500 × $1.50 = $8,250
Budgeted Overhead = $3,000 + $(.90) (6,000) = $8,400

(When this method is used, the budget authorization is based on *actual* direct labor.)

Underabsorbed Overhead = $8,600 − $8,250 = $350

The overhead variance of $350 unfavorable is divided as follows:

Volume Variance = The actual volume times the absorption rate minus the budgeted amount at actual volume = (6,000 × $1.50) − $8,400 = $600 favorable volume variance.

Spending Variance = Budgeted amount at actual volume minus actual overhead cost = $8,400 − $8,600 = $200 unfavorable spending variance.

Efficiency Variance = Standard hours times the absorption rate minus the actual hours times the absorption rate = (5,500 × $1.50) − (6,000 × $1.50) = $750 unfavorable.

Summary:

Volume = $600 favorable
Spending = 200 unfavorable
Efficiency = 750 unfavorable

NET = $350 unfavorable

There is usually little use for this type of overhead variance analysis. The plant manager is generally responsible for both the spending and efficiency variance and little, if anything, is accomplished by separating them. The only thing that this analysis accomplishes is to isolate that part of the overhead variance that results from off-standard direct labor. This might have some use if there were different persons responsible for direct labor and variable overhead. This is practically never true. In any case, the increase in overhead resulting from an hour of off-standard direct labor is usually considerably different from the standard overhead cost per hour. For example, it is quite possible for off-standard direct labor to cause an increase only in fringe benefits. To the extent that this is true, the amounts calculated using the above method will be incorrect.

THE USE OF VARIANCE ANALYSIS

The purpose of variance analysis is to provide management with information about off-standard cost conditions. This information should be such that management can use it for making decisions. Variance analysis should be kept as simple as possible within this limitation. Complex analyses of variances should be made only when there is a positive reason for so doing because the more complex the variance analysis, the more difficult it frequently is for management to understand. In the Birmingham Chemical Works, for example, there should be a positive reason for breaking out mix and usage variance. If management cannot control either variance, a total figure would be sufficient. Also, as already indicated, the analysis of overhead variance into spending and efficiency variance is usually not worth while.

Even in the case of the simpler analyses, it is not always useful to break out variances in the detail described. For example, in many companies the rate variance will always result from a man working out of his classification (for example, a toolmaker at $3.00 an hour running a centerless grinder normally run by an operator at $2.00 an hour). When labor rates are subject to union negotiation and are only changed infrequently, the actual and budgeted rate will always be the same. If the rates are changed, the standards are also usually changed. Both efficiency and rate will be, therefore, the responsibility of the foreman and there is little use in reporting them separately.

If, however, there is a valid use for some variance information, it should be provided. The student is often misled with respect to the cost of a complex variance analysis because of the time it takes *him* to make the calculations. This time is considerably shorter in an actual business situation. Once the procedure has been set up and worksheets prepared, the calculation of variances is a clerical job that can be handled quite easily with desk calculators. If the cost analyses are handled by an electronic computer, the marginal cost of additional variance information may be insignificant.

SUMMARY

A variance is the difference between actual and standard cost. For convenience of explanation in this chapter, variance analyses have been divided into two types: simple and complex. Simple variance analysis occurs when changes in the Work-in-Process Inventory can be ignored and when each type of variance (material, labor, and overhead) is subdivided only into two kinds. Complex variance analysis occurs when changes in the Work-in-Process Inventory must be taken into account or where each type of variance is subdivided into more than two kinds.

The purpose of variance analysis is to provide management with information about off-standard costs. Variance analysis should be extended only insofar as the additional information is useful to management. If management cannot make a decision on the basis of a variance, it is questionable whether this information should be provided. The cost of obtaining the information is usually not the reason for a simplified variance analysis. The reason is that variance information upon which no decision can be made is, at best, useless and may even be confusing to management.

CHAPTER THREE

The Allocation of Costs

In cost accounting rarely will all of the manufacturing costs applicable to a product be identified directly with that product. (About the only time this will occur is in a one-product plant where all costs incurred in the plant must be applicable to that one product.) All cost accounting systems, therefore, require some allocation of costs among the products produced. The techniques for allocating costs can have a significant influence on the information generated by the cost accounting system; consequently, careful consideration should be given to the kind of allocation techniques that are used. (Because material and direct labor can, by definition, be assigned directly to a product, the cost allocation techniques apply only to overhead costs.)

A cost allocation assigns a common cost to two or more departments or products. The objective is to assign a "fair share" of the costs to the product or department by allocating the costs in proportion to the relative responsibility for their incidence. The purpose of a system of cost allocation is to assign all of the indirect costs of manufacturing to some product in order to obtain an estimate of the "total" cost of the product.

Manufacturing overhead costs are assigned to products as follows:

1. Assign all possible overhead costs directly to the department responsible. Such costs normally include the indirect labor working

in the department, supplies used by the department, and depreciation of the equipment in the department.

2. Allocate all general plant costs (such as building depreciation, building repairs, or electricity and water [to the extent they are not metered by department]) to the service and production departments using them. The allocation should be based on the most "equitable" measure of usage that is available.

3. Allocate the service department costs to the productive departments, to the extent practicable on the basis of services performed.

4. Allocate the departmental overhead costs to the product.

ALLOCATION BASES

Common Bases of Allocation

Following is a list of general plant costs and service departments with some common bases for allocation:

Cost or Department	Allocation Basis
Building depreciation	Relative floor space occupied
Building maintenance and repairs	Relative floor space occupied
Rent	Relative floor space occupied
Heat and light	Relative floor space occupied
Property taxes and insurance	Relative floor space occupied
Power (if not metered to department)	Relative horsepower of equipment
Taxes and insurance on machinery	Relative book value of machinery and equipment
Maintenance	Time spent by maintenance men or value of equipment in department
Water and steam (if not metered to department)	Analysis of departmental requirements (i.e., special studies of usage)
Laboratory	Relative number of jobs performed or relative time spent on jobs for each department
Industrial relations department	Relative number of people
Plant superintendent	Relative direct labor dollars
Miscellaneous plant costs	Relative direct labor dollars
Payroll department	Relative number of people
Accounting department	Relative value of production

It can be seen that many of these methods of cost allocation are arbitrary and the idea of "fair share" becomes rather tenuous.

Deciding Which Bases to Use

In deciding which bases of cost allocation to use, it is useful to separate the costs to be allocated into three groups, as follows:

1. Those costs that can be controlled by the department manager using the service.
2. Those costs which, although not directly controllable by the department manager, are more or less variable with the level of production.
3. Those costs that are neither controllable by the department manager nor variable with the level of production.

The value of separating the costs in this manner is that it makes evident which costs require extra care in the determination of an allocation method. Where the department can control the level of the expense, it is important to have an allocation method that will motivate the department manager to keep these expenses under careful control. Perhaps the best example of this occurs with respect to maintenance cost. A department foreman frequently can exercise considerable control over the level of this expense. If he is allocated a share of the total maintenance cost based on, for example, the book value of the machinery and equipment in his department, he has little incentive to schedule his maintenance efficiently because he is charged approximately the same amount no matter how much maintenance his department has incurred. If, however, maintenance costs are allocated on the basis of the hours of maintenance time actually devoted to his department, he would be motivated to use the maintenance men judiciously.

The second category of allocated cost varies with the volume of production. It is important to allocate this expense as precisely as possible so that the variable product cost can be determined with a reasonable degree of accuracy. For example, a considerable part of power expense will usually vary with the volume of production. In calculating product cost, it is important that this expense be reflected as a variable cost. If, power is allocated to the department on some arbitrary basis (such as rated horsepower of equipment), the cost would not vary with volume at the departmental level. If Department A, for instance, had 30 per cent of the total rated horsepower in the plant, it would be allocated 30 per cent of the power costs. If, however, Department A worked at 50 per cent of capacity during a particular month and the rest of the plant worked at 100 per cent, 30 per cent of the total power bill would not be a reasonable allocation. The use of standard costs at standard volume will overcome the objection that variable costs may not be stated correctly. There is still a problem, however, in that the variance from standard with respect to power is meaningless. The allocated costs will be a function of total plant production rather than the production in the department.

Usually, where an allocated cost varies with volume, it is quite easy to find a basis for determining a department's "fair share." (In the case of power, water, steam, for example, it is the actual amount used.) It is, however, sometimes a problem to find an inexpensive method for measuring this "share." It may not be practical, for example, to meter water, steam, or power by department. If the total amount of the expense is relatively small, a more or less fixed allocation will do no harm. It is important, however, to recognize this situation so that the departmental overhead rates will reflect these costs as variable.

The third type of cost allocations, of necessity, are arbitrary and there is usually little to choose between alternative methods. These costs are allocated to product to provide management with an approximation of total costs, and management should understand that the fixed portion of the unit cost is only a rough approximation.

One method to test the reasonableness of a particular system of allocation is to try several combinations. All reasonable combinations should give approximately the same answers. To decide which of the possible combinations gives the most reliable results, ask: "Which method provides differences in unit costs between the products best reflecting the differentials that might exist if each product were produced in its own plant?" Unit cost differentials should result from differences in such things as design, quality, or production techniques rather than from the vagaries of the cost allocation system.

ALLOCATING SERVICE DEPARTMENT COSTS
TO PRODUCTIVE DEPARTMENTS

There are two principal procedures for allocating service department costs to productive departments: (1) allocate the service department cost to productive departments only; (2) allocate the service department cost to other service departments as well as to productive departments. (The first procedure was described briefly in Chapter 1.)

Under the first procedure: (1) decide on a basis for allocating the costs of each service department (as described in the previous section); (2) allocate the costs of each service department directly to the productive departments on these bases.

Under the second procedure, service department costs are allocated as follows:

(1) Decide on a method for allocating the cost of each service department to the other departments.

(2) Place the service departments in the order that they are to be closed out.

This order is based on the amount of service that a department *renders* to other service departments as compared to the amount of services that it *receives*. The first department to be closed out is the one with the greatest net amount of service rendered to other service departments. The next department to be closed will be the one rendering the second greatest net amount of service to other service departments, and so on, until the last service department, which will be the one *receiving* the most service. (A general approximation of this order is all that is required.)

(3) Close the service departments to the productive departments.

The first service department on the list of departments will be closed to all of the other departments, service as well as production. The second department on the list will be closed to *all* departments except the first one (and, of course, the department being closed). This will be continued until all service departments have been closed to the productive departments. The bases for allocating the service departments' costs will usually be the same as if the service departments were allocated directly to productive departments. In some cases, however, the fact that the service departments' costs are being allocated to other service departments may require a change in allocation base. For example, the plant manager's office cannot be allocated on the basis of relative direct labor costs because the service departments have no direct labor; therefore, the allocation base will have to be total labor dollars.

ALLOCATION OF DEPARTMENT COST TO PRODUCT

The objective of allocating departmental overhead costs to product is similar to the objective of allocating service department costs to productive departments; that is, the goal is to assign a "fair share" of the departmental overhead to each of the products produced in the department. The usual basis is direct labor—either hours or dollars—because direct labor is generally assumed to be the best measure of the relative amount of overhead required to produce a part. It is reasoned that direct labor will be proportional to the amount of machine time applicable to the product and, therefore, the amount of machine costs (such as maintenance and depreciation); it will be a measure of the relative amount of indirect labor applicable to the product; it will also be a measure of the relative amount of fringe benefits applicable to the product. In general, this is a reasonably accurate statement of conditions and accounts for the fact that direct labor is the most common allocation base.

It should be noted that direct labor is used as a basis for allocation because it is proportional to the amount of overhead generated by producing the product. It is not used because direct labor *generates* this overhead. This is an important distinction and should be constantly kept in mind when using cost accounting data. If a department having an overhead rate of 200 per cent adds direct labor cost (for example, on-line inspection) of $.50 per unit to a product, it does not mean that overhead costs will increase $1.00 per unit, although the accounting system may reflect it this way. (This point will be covered in more detail in Chapter 5.)

The increase in the degree of automation in many industries has made direct labor a less reliable basis for allocating overhead to product than it was several years ago. In the 1920's and 1930's an overhead rate of 50 per cent was common because direct labor constituted such a large portion of the total manufacturing costs. Today a 50 per cent overhead rate frequently covers only the fringe benefits applicable to the direct labor. Overhead rates of 300 per cent to 400 per cent are common and rates of 1,000 per cent or even 2,000 per cent are not unknown. In most instances, the reliability of direct labor as a basis of allocation tends to vary inversely with the size of the burden rate. At the present time, the direct labor basis of allocation is already obsolete in many companies and every indication suggests this trend continuing in the future.

Machine hours are an alternative basis for allocating departmental overhead to product. The use of a machine-hour basis of overhead allocation, however, requires a more complex calculation. An overhead rate based on direct labor requires only that the total departmental overhead be divided by total departmental direct labor. If the overhead rate is based on machine hours, however, it is necessary to allocate all of the department cost to machine or group of similar machines. (This is fairly straightforward for maintenance, depreciation, power, or taxes. It may be quite arbitrary, however, for indirect labor, supplies, or scrap.) The overhead cost of each machine or group of machines is divided by the total hours of operation to obtain a cost per hour. This rate is then applied to the number of machine hours required to produce the product.

Although it is possible to obtain "actual" costs using the machine-hour method, it is usually used as part of a standard cost system. A standard cost per machine hour is calculated on the basis of budgeted overhead allocated to machine hours at standard volume. The standard cost per machine hour is then applied to the standard number of machine hours per unit to obtain the standard overhead cost per unit.

The use of a machine rate for overhead allocation has several disadvantages. As already stated, it requires an additional allocation process to determine standard machine rates. In doing this, some of the costs must be allocated to machine in a fairly arbitrary fashion. Another disadvantage is that unit costs can be distorted by arbitrary differences in the values of the equipment. For example, if Product A is produced by Machine Number 1, purchased in 1939, and if Product B, nearly identical to A, is produced by Machine Number 2, purchased in 1959, depreciation, taxes and insurance will normally be much higher on Machine 2 and the cost of Product B will be higher as a result. Higher maintenance costs on Machine Number 1 may partially offset the higher depreciation, but this would be only a coincidence.

Product and pricing decisions on A and B could be distorted if the standard costs of these two nearly identical products were different. Management might be led to believe (and, worse, act upon this belief) that A was more profitable than B. This would be particularly embarrassing if Machine 1 could produce either A or B (a not uncommon situation) and just the "luck of the draw" resulted in Product B being produced on Machine 2 and Product A being produced on Machine 1. The disadvantage of differences in the book value of different machines is overcome at the department level when a single overhead rate is used for the entire department, as is usual when direct labor is used as the basis for allocating overhead to the products. (The problem can still exist *between* departments, however, as will be explained later.)

In spite of the problems, the use of machine hours is the best choice in many cases. Where the costs that are directly related to equipment are high compared with direct labor and other overhead (as in automated plants) and where the equipment is generally comparable in age and efficiency, machine hours will provide the best method for allocating overhead to product. The validity of any method is, in the final analysis, measured by the validity of the results. Accordingly, the validity of machine hours as an allocation basis can be tested by analyzing the results. Do cost differentials among products reflect differences in such things as design and quality, or are they related to the particular equipment used in producing the parts? If it is the former, machine hours is an adequate basis of allocation; if it is the latter, it is not.

A third type of allocation base that is sometimes used is direct material (or prime costs [material and direct labor] which is a variation of this method). Material should only be used as a basis for allocation where the *overhead costs are closely related to the value of material.* Simply because material represents a large portion of the total manufacturing cost does not in itself make it a reliable base. If a plant assembles semimanufactured components into finished products, the value of these components will be inversely proportional to the amount of overhead required to complete them. The more complete the component, the higher will be the purchase price, but the smaller the cost to complete at the plant. For example, Part A is purchased complete for $5.00; Part B is semifinished for $3.00. B requires $.50 of direct labor to complete. If material is used as a basis for allocation, the finished product that included Part A will be assessed more burden than the product that included Part B. In view of the additional manufacturer costs applicable to Part B, this is clearly incorrect.

Another method for assigning burden to part is to determine a burden rate by type of operation, without regard to the department in which the part is produced. For example, the operations of a factory can be subdivided into the following types: fully automated machining; semi-automated machining; nonautomated machining; heavy assembly; and light assembly. The relation of burden cost to the direct labor cost for each type of operation can be estimated and these percentages adjusted so that all of the budgeted overhead will be absorbed at standard volume. Unit overhead costs are calculated by applying these rates to the labor cost for each type of operation.

In general, the direct labor base has several advantages over the other bases described and should be used where it provides comparable results. First, the direct labor method of allocating overhead is widely used and, consequently, better understood by management. Second, it usually requires less clerical work. For example, the overhead absorbed during a month can be calculated by multiplying the departmental burden rates by the standard direct labor incurred (a figure that should always be available). Other methods generally involve multiplying the standard unit burden amount applicable to each part by the number of parts produced and adding the results. In automated plants, however, it may well be worthwhile to undertake the extra work involved in using some base other than direct labor. The question to be answered is: Does the alternative method provide a unit cost that is more useful than the unit cost using a direct labor base?

DISTORTIONS IN UNIT COSTS

There are two situations in cost determination that frequently cause a distortion in product costs: one results from differences in the book value of equipment among departments or plants; the second results from differences in the capacity utilized among departments or plants.

Book Value of Equipment

This problem can best be demonstrated by an example. An automobile company has two engine plants, one producing eight-cylinder engines, the other six-cylinder engines. The six-cylinder engines are pro-

duced in a plant built in the 1920's; the eight-cylinder engines are produced in a plant built in the early 1950's. In order to help decide on an
equitable selling price differential, the standard cost (it might have been
actual) of each engine was calculated. These standard costs turned out
to be worthless as a basis for making a decision on the price differentials.
The six-cylinder engine plant had very low depreciation and low fixed
investment per unit (the company used a rate of return on investment
for the profit markup). The eight-cylinder engine plant, on the other
hand, had high depreciation and investment. Although the new equipment was more efficient, it did not offset the higher depreciation and
profit markup resulting from the higher investment in new equipment.

The differential in variable cost could not be used because the eight-
cylinder engine plant had *lower* variable manufacturing costs (excluding material). It was clear to everyone, however, that the eight-cylinder
engine would cost more to produce than the six-cylinder engine if they
were both produced on comparable facilities. The situation was further
complicated by the fact that a new six-cylinder engine plant would
have to be built in the near future because of capacity limitations on the
old equipment and because of anticipated changes in the design of the
six-cylinder engine.

In this case, the price differential should have been based on the
difference between the cost to produce the eight-cylinder engine in the
new plant and the estimated cost to produce the six-cylinder engine in
a comparable plant. This differential is known in the automobile business
as the "designed" cost differential. It means the cost that has been "designed into a product" and is used to approximate the "worth" to the
customer. This is a very important distinction that must be made when
using cost data for pricing decisions. The age of the plant producing a
part is of no interest to a customer. The fact that he has a six-cylinder
engine is. It is irrational, therefore, to use a cost differential that includes
the factor of age of plant to decide how much to charge the customer
for a product.

If the price differential is determined by competition, there is still
the problem of product line profitability. The selling price minus total
costs might show the eight-cylinder engines much less profitable than
the six. The same price minus the variable costs would show that the
eight-cylinder engine earned a higher contribution. Yet, the price differential might reflect the precise difference in the designed cost between the two products.

This example demonstrates an exaggerated condition and one where
the unadjusted accounting data clearly cannot be used. If, however, the
distortion in costs had been on a much smaller scale, it may not have
been detected. In another actual case, Product A was made in Depart-

ments 1, 2, and 3; Product B was made in Departments 1, 2, and 4. The equipment in Department 4 had been purchased postwar, while the equipment in Department 3 had been purchased prewar. Because of the difference in depreciation and investment, Product A showed a much higher rate of profit on investment than Product B. There was a feeling among the executives of the company that Product B was priced too low and that if the price could not be raised, plans should be made to stop production on Product B and expand the production of A. A study showed that the entire profit differential resulted from the difference in investment. (As a matter of fact, B would have been slightly more profitable than A if produced in Department 3.)

In most cases, this type of situation will have little or no effect on management decisions and need not be corrected (except to stop showing meaningless figures to management). The point to consider is that the effect of differences in the book value of equipment can have a much greater impact on product cost than the methods of allocating service costs to productive department or departmental costs to product line. In evaluating product line profits, it is something that should always be kept in mind.

Relative Capacity

A situation similar to the book value problem can occur when the departments of a plant (or the plants of a company) work at different levels of capacity. For example, a company produces three grades of paper. Grades 1 and 2 go through all departments except the large beater and mixer departments. Grade 3 goes through all departments except the small beater and mixer departments. All departments work at about 90 per cent of capacity except the large beater and mixer departments which work at 50 per cent of capacity. The costs of grade 3 will be relatively higher than grades 1 and 2 because of the greater excess capacity costs assigned to grade 3. Grade 3 will show a smaller profit and return on investment because of this. In this case, also, management can be misled into believing that the selling price is too low or that perhaps this line should be abandoned.

In this problem, as in the book value problem, there may be no practical way to correct the situation. In any event, it is important for the controller and manager to know when this condition exists so that no incorrect management action is taken. Here also, differences in the relative level of operations among departments can have a greater effect on the product cost than the methods of allocation.

SUMMARY

If product costs are to be calculated, a cost allocation is required where manufacturing costs are common to more than one product. The objective in making a cost allocation is to assign a "fair share" of the costs of production to the products. A "fair share" may be defined as the relative amount of cost that each of the products would have generated had they been produced separately. There are two types of cost allocations that are used in most cost accounting systems: (1) general plant costs and service department cost to productive department; (2) productive department costs to the products produced in the department.

It is useful to divide service department allocations into three groups: (1) costs over which the productive department managers can exercise control; (2) costs that are variable with the level of production but over which productive department management has little control; (3) costs that are not controllable by the productive department manager and that do not vary with volume.

Although it is important that care be taken in selecting methods for allocating costs, frequently other situations can create greater problems than the bases for allocation. One of these problems occurs when departments or plants have equipment purchased at different price levels. The other occurs when departments and plants work at different levels of capacity.

CHAPTER FOUR

Joint and By-Product Cost Accounting

Where a business produces joint products or by-products, it is important to recognize this condition in the cost accounting system. The existence of joint products makes some traditional cost accounting techniques useless. Worse, in some cases, the use of certain cost accounting techniques that, under usual circumstances, are correct may lead management to make incorrect decisions. It is of primary importance, therefore, that the cost accounting and control system be designed to take care of the unique problems of joint products. The special accounting problems presented by joint production, together with methods for solving these problems, are considered in this chapter.

JOINT PRODUCTS DEFINED

Joint production occurs whenever two or more products *must* result from the same production process. The key word in this definition is "must." The crucial characteristic of joint products is that *the production of one automatically results in the production of the others*. It is often possible, of course, to eliminate one of the joint products; it is not economic to do so if the product has a sales value greater than the unique

46

costs of completing and marketing. For example, in marble quarrying, it is possible to leave all the marble except the best at the quarry site. If other grades must be quarried to obtain the best grade, it is not economic to leave the other grades at the quarry so long as their sales value exceeds the unique costs of finishing and selling. In this case, the quarrying of marble is a joint-production process because, in quarrying pure white marble, it is necessary (from an economic point of view) to quarry other grades.

The fact that joint products *must* be produced together is of major importance to the cost accountant because it means that all *cost allocations among joint products are entirely arbitrary.* If two products must result from a single productive process, one product cannot be had without the other. If it is not possible to have one product without both, the cost of producing only one cannot be isolated. The facts are that it costs a certain sum of money to produce a certain amount of each of two products. If part of the joint-production cost is assigned to one of the products, it is a meaningless allocation. This is the most important thing to remember about joint cost accounting because it is this characteristic that makes it necessary to modify traditional cost accounting techniques.

JOINT COSTS AND COMMON COSTS

There is an important difference between joint costs and common costs. Common costs occur when two products that may be produced separately are produced together. For example, when several products are made in different departments of the same plant, the plant costs (such as plant maintenance and depreciation) are common. Common costs differ from joint costs in that the *production of common parts can be undertaken separately.* Because the production of one part does not mean that the other part must be produced, the cost accountant is able to estimate the costs of producing any of the parts individually. Depending on the degree of accuracy required, the cost determination may include several more or less arbitrary allocations. Nevertheless, it is at least theoretically possible to allocate costs in such a way that the costs of each of the common products will approximate the relative costs of these products if they were produced separately or in other combinations. This is not true of joint products, since they cannot be produced separately and can be produced only in limited (and frequently noncontrollable) other combinations.

The unit costs of common products are useful in making pricing decisions or in determining product-line profitability; however, in joint products, unit costs are meaningless for determining the adequacy of price levels or the profitability of product lines. The relevant figures for decision-making are the total price and the total profit of all of the joint products.

METHODS OF ALLOCATING JOINT COSTS

If it were not for inventories, there would be no reason for estimating the costs of each of the joint products at all. On the income statement the total cost of the joint products would be subtracted from the total revenue without regard to product line. Inventories do exist in most companies, however, and a value must be placed on these inventories. Inventory values are generally obtained by allocating the joint costs of production to the joint products. In allocating these costs, the overriding consideration is that they should be allocated in such a way that management, using the information, will not be led into making incorrect decisions. These incorrect decisions can take two forms:

1. Management may discontinue producing and marketing a joint product that should be retained; or
2. Management may continue to produce and market a joint product that should be discontinued.

The first mistake can occur if management is given information on profits by product. A joint product may show an accounted loss and, unless the nature of joint costs are known, management may wish to discontinue production of the unprofitable product. Profits by product should, therefore, never be shown to management because at best they are meaningless and, at worst, they could lead to an incorrect decision. (Methods for preventing the second mistake are treated under By-Product Accounting.)

In deciding on a procedure for allocating the joint costs of production, it is important to consider the effect that this procedure will have on the cost and financial statements and, consequently, on management decisions. The most common mistake accountants make is to show profit by product line, somewhat as follows:

	Joint Product A	Joint Product B	Joint Product C	Total
Sales	$10,000	$5,000	$4,000	$19,000
Joint Cost of Production (a)	7,000	3,500	2,800	13,300
Gross Profit	$ 3,000	$1,500	$1,200	$ 5,700
Unique Costs of Production	2,000	1,000	300	3,300
Selling and Admin. Expense	1,000	800	200	2,000
NET PROFIT	$ 0	$ (300)	$ 700	$ 400

(a) Calculated in accordance with the market price method described in the next section.

Management receiving a statement such as this would be justified in believing that Product A earned no profit, Product B sustained a loss of $300, and Product C earned $700. *This is not the case at all.* The only profit fact that the accountant possesses is that the total profit on all joint products is $400. Nothing is accomplished by breaking down profits further except the confusion of management.

In evaluating a method for allocating the joint costs of production to the joint products, the question to ask is, How will the financial statements be affected by this method? A satisfactory method should result in no incorrect or misleading information appearing in the financial statements or accounting reports. Three methods for allocating joint costs are described in the following pages. In each case, these methods will be evaluated in terms of their effects upon the financial statements of the company.

Average Method

The average method, as the name implies, involves assigning the same average cost to each unit produced. The unit is usually a quantity such as a pound, ton, gallon, board foot, or cubic foot. For example, in petroleum refining, the total joint costs of "cracking" the petroleum can be assigned to the joint products by dividing the joint costs by the number of gallons in the yield. Each of the products will then be valued for inventory purposes at the average joint cost per gallon plus the unique costs, if any. Or in marble quarrying, the cost of quarrying the marble can be divided by the cubic feet of marble quarried. The inventory would then be valued at the average cost per cubic foot of marble.

The average method of joint-costing can only be used when the selling prices of each of the joint products are about equal after adjusting for the unique costs. If it is used where there are significant differences in the selling prices of the finished product, the income statement can be seriously distorted by difference in the sales mix of the joint products.

To take an extreme example, a meat packer might value all of the products from a steer at the average cost. If he purchased a 2,000-pound steer for $200, his average cost per pound would be $.10. Thus a pound of steak would be valued at $.10 and a pound of bone would have the same value. If he had no inventory (or if the inventory were always perfectly balanced [that is, proportion to the yield]) the total income would not be distorted. (Under these conditions, it is unnecessary to value individual products.) If, however, the inventory varied from month to month, income could be seriously distorted. If a steer were purchased and butchered in January and all of the steak (but none of the other products) were sold that month, January profits would be very high because the selling price of the steak would be offset by a cost of only $.10 a pound. In February, however, when the bones and other waste products were sold, the income statement would show a loss.

When the accountant explains to management the reason for the differences in profit between the two months, he must do so in terms of the difference in the profitability of the joint products. Even though product-line profits are not shown separately on the income statement, the arbitrary differences in profits (resulting from the average method of allocating joint costs) are reflected in the income statement. *The possible effect on profits from changes in product mix is an important consideration in deciding which method of allocation to use.*

In addition to the possibility of profit distortion, the average method of valuing joint products is also questionable accounting practice. On the "lower of cost or market" rule the value of the inventories of the lower priced products will be overstated and, consequently, it will be necessary to write them down. This will result in a significant undervaluation of inventory because the high-price products will continue to be understated.

The only advantage of the average method is ease of calculation. Even here, other more satisfactory methods are not a great deal more work. As a rule of thumb, any time the average method is used, the possible undesirable effect on the cost and income statements should be considered carefully.

Market Price Method

The market price method of allocating joint costs is computed as follows:

1. Calculate the total cost of the joint production up to the point that the products are *separated*. (This includes labor and overhead as well as material.)
2. Calculate the total sales value of the joint products. This is done by multiplying the number of units of each product by the selling price and adding the resulting amounts.
3. Divide the amount in (1) by the amount in (2). This is the percentage of cost to selling price.
4. To find the joint cost of any product, multiply the unit selling price by the percentage in (3).
5. Add any *unique* production costs to the joint costs calculated in (4).

EXAMPLE OF JOINT COST CALCULATION

JOINT COSTS OF PRODUCTION

Material	$50,000
Labor	10,000
Overhead	20,000
TOTAL	$80,000

UNITS PRODUCED AND SELLING PRICES

Product	Number Units Produced (a)	Selling Price	Units in Ending Inventory
A	10,000	$10.00	100
B	25,000	1.00	500
C	80,000	.10	10,000

(a) This can be any production period from a single batch up to a year's production. The important condition is that the mix of products be typical of the joint-production yield.

Required: Calculate the value of the ending inventory.

1. Total costs of production = $80,000
2. Total sales value = 10,000 × $10.00 = $100,000
   25,000 × $ 1.00 = 25,000
   80,000 × $ .10 = 8,000

   TOTAL $133,000

3. The percentage of cost of sales = $\dfrac{80,000}{133,000}$ = 60%

4. The value of the ending inventory is calculated as follows:

Product	Cost	Volume	Total Value
A	$6.00	100	$600
B	.60	500	300
C	.06	10,000	600
TOTAL			$1,500

The principal advantage of the market price method from a management accounting point of view is that gross profit as a per cent of the sales dollar is the same for all products. This minimizes the effect on the monthly income statements of changes in the sales mix of the joint products. In the meat packing example the gross profit of all products will be the same percentage of sales, using the market price method. The monthly income statement will not, therefore, show high profits when the steaks are sold and losses when the other products are sold.

Another advantage of the market price method is that it provides inventory values that are generally acceptable to the public accountant. For this reason, probably more than any other, the market price method is the one most commonly used.

It should be noted, however, that the market price method does not provide product costs for determining product-line profits. It is useful only to value inventories. The method is recommended because it minimizes distortion in the income statement. The costs have no further significance and product costs calculated using this method are as arbitrary as the product costs obtained using the average method. Remember that the cardinal rule in joint cost accounting is: *Never show product-line profits.*

Modified Market Price Method

Sometimes, even using the market price method, the income may change between periods because of differences in the sales mix of the joint products. This occurs when the distribution costs of the joint products are significantly different. The following problem illustrates this:

	Joint Product A	Joint Product B
Quantities	15,000 lbs.	5,000 lbs.
Selling Price	$5.00	$3.00
Joint Production Cost (a)	3.00	1.80
Unique Selling Costs	1.00	2.00

(a) Total selling price = $90,000; joint-production costs = $54,000; cost as a per cent of sales = 60%.

The sale of these items from inventory will result in a $1.00 accounted profit for A and an $.80 accounted loss for B. If the relative sales of products A and B differ significantly from month to month, profits will be affected. The only explanation is that the sales mix is different. This implies to management that there is a difference between the profitability of the two products. Because this cannot be true (remember that the joint-production costs allocation is strictly arbitrary), management has every reason to feel confused.

This problem can be solved by taking the market price method a step beyond the gross profit and carrying it to the net profit. In the example above, the joint cost of production could be allocated to equate the net profit of the two products as a percentage of the sales dollar. This is done as follows:

1. Calculate the total sales dollars that would be received from the joint production, by product.

2. Subtract the estimated unique selling costs from the sales dollars, by product.
3. Subtract the joint costs of production from figures obtained in (2). (This is net profit.)
4. Calculate the per cent of net profit to sales for the total only.
5. Apply the percentage in (4) to the sales by product, and subtract this amount from the amount obtained in (2). This is the joint cost of production.
6. Divide the amounts obtained in (5) by the number of units produced, by product. This is the allocated joint cost per unit.

In the above example, the calculation is as follows:

	Product A	Product B	Total
a. Sales dollars	$75,000 [a]	$15,000 [b]	$90,000
b. Unique selling costs	15,000	10,000	25,000
c. Revenue in excess of selling costs	$60,000	$5,000	$65,000
d. Joint costs			54,000
e. Net profit—distributed to product as a per cent of sales (12.2%)	9,150	1,850	$11,000
f. Total joint cost of production	$50,850	$3,150	
g. Joint costs per unit	$3.39	$.63	

[a] 15,000 units @ $5.00 per unit.
[b] 5,000 units @ $3.00 per unit.

Notice that the modified market price method equates net profit as a per cent of the sales dollar between the joint products. (The market price method equates *gross profit* as a per cent of the sales dollar.) It is also possible to equate net or gross profit per unit among the joint products. This may be confusing to management, however, because most managers tend to relate profit to dollar sales rather than unit sales.

The modified market price method is preferable to the market price method where:

1. The unique distribution costs of the joint products differ significantly; and
2. The mix of product sales differs significantly between accounting periods.

(As explained under By-Product Accounting, this method also has an advantage in certain cases in accounting for by-product costs.) If these two conditions do not exist, the more traditional market price method is probably better because it is somewhat easier to calculate and people are generally more familiar with it.

BY-PRODUCT ACCOUNTING

From an accounting viewpoint, a by-product is merely a joint product that is treated in a special way. The profit from the sale of the by-product is subtracted from the joint costs of production. By-product treatment is generally accorded to the products from the joint-production processes having relatively small sales revenue. With respect to by-product accounting, there are two main problems:

1. Which products should be treated as by-products?
2. How should the by-product inventory be valued?

Traditional By-Product Method

Earlier, it was pointed out that there were two mistakes that management can make with respect to joint products:

1. Discontinue completing and marketing a product that is providing a contribution; and
2. Continue to complete and market a product where the unique costs exceed the selling price.

As already stated, the first mistake can be avoided by omitting profits by individual products. The second mistake can be avoided by treating as by-products all products where there is a possibility that the unique costs may exceed the selling price. The traditional by-product cost accounting technique is to subtract the net sales revenue of the by-product from the joint costs of production. (The net sales revenue is the selling price minus the unique costs.) Consequently, the traditional by-product cost accounting provides a mechanism for systematically comparing revenue to unique costs. If, whenever a possibility exists that the unique costs will exceed the revenue, a product is treated as a by-product, management can be assured that no such products will be produced without being informed of this fact.

The answer to the question of which products should be treated as by-products is: *All products where unique costs may exceed the selling price.*

UNIQUE COSTS

Unique costs include both fixed and variable costs. That is, if machinery and equipment are required to complete the production of a by-product (or a joint product), the depreciation from the machinery is included in the unique costs. If, however, total unique costs exceed the selling price, it will also be necessary to know the variable cost before a decision can be made. (It will probably not be necessary to calculate variable unique costs on a regular basis because this information is only needed when the total unique costs exceed the selling price.)

It should be noted that because the unique costs exceed the selling price, it does not follow in all cases that the product must be discontinued. It does mean, that the advisability of such a move be considered. For example, management might decide to continue to sell a product temporarily, at an out-of-pocket loss to maintain marketing channels.

Modified Market Price Method

The modified market price method, described earlier in the chapter, may be used instead of the traditional by-product accounting technique to protect management from producing goods at an out-of-pocket loss. This method makes it quickly evident whether the unique costs of any of the joint products exceed the selling price because, when inventory values are calculated, these products show a *negative contribution*.

The modified market price method has the following advantages, in addition to providing a systematic comparison of unique costs to selling prices:

1. It is not necessary to separate joint products from by-products because all are treated the same.
2. It provides the least distortion in the income statements from changes in product mix.

Inventory Valuation

Using the traditional by-product treatment, inventories of by-products can be valued as follows:

a. Selling price
b. Selling price minus unique costs
c. Unique costs
d. No value

In this case, as in the case of joint products, the situation to be avoided is changes in profit because of difference in the sales mix. In the case of by-products, the values are usually so small that profits are relatively unaffected regardless of the method used to value inventories. In deciding which of the four methods to use, estimate the effect that each would have on profits, assuming the maximum likely swing in the mix of by-product sales. Other things being equal, the method that has the smallest effect on net profits is the one to use. If all appear to have a significant effect on profits, using the modified market price method should be considered.

STANDARD COSTS AND JOINT PRODUCT ACCOUNTING

Joint cost processes are almost always adaptable to the use of standard costs. Joint cost production generally involves processing some raw material into two or more finished products. The only difference between a joint-product cost accounting system and a traditional process cost accounting system is that unit cost calculations are for inventory valuation only; product line profits are meaningless. Otherwise, a standard cost system would be identical with one involving the processing of only one product (or several products not produced jointly).

In a standard cost system, inventories of the joint products are valued at standard joint cost. The calculation of standard joint cost is exactly the same as described previously except that forecast selling prices, standard yields, and standard costs of production are used instead of actuals. (Note, also, that standard joint costs can be average, market price, or modified market price.)

JOINT COST WHERE OUTPUT IS CONTROLLABLE

Where some control can be exercised over the mix of products that result from a joint production process, the cost accountant has additional responsibilities. He must give management information that will help in making decisions to maximize the profitability of the joint products. (Note, however, that the calculation of joint costs will be made in the same manner. The only thing that will be affected will be the mix of the joint products.)

In most cases, profits will be maximized when revenue is maximized. That is, as much of the higher-price products as possible should be produced. If, however, the unique costs are different among the joint products, this may not be true. The products to produce are those that provide the greatest contribution over unique costs, in distribution as well as production.

In many cases, the relative contribution of the different joint products can be calculated once and used thereafter, with only an annual review. This occurs when the order of profitability is unlikely to be changed. In other cases, where selling prices or unique costs vary, it may be necessary to prepare weekly estimates of relative contribution to guide the engineers in determining the output.

The cost accountant must do two additional things when the product mix in joint production is controllable:

1. Give management the relative contribution of each of the joint products;
2. Provide this information as often as is required for making operating decisions.

SUMMARY

Joint production occurs whenever two or more products *must* be produced together. Joint production creates a unique cost accounting problem: *it is impossible to get meaningful costs of the individual joint products*. The objective of the joint cost accounting system is to provide management with meaningful data. Since the cost of the individual joint product is meaningless, no product-line profit should be reported to management. It is necessary, however, to place a value on joint products when they are retained in inventory. This is usually done by using the market price method of allocating costs. If, however, the unique costs of distributing the joint products are significantly different, this method could result in distorting monthly profits when the product mix varies from month to month. This problem can be avoided by using the modified market price method. This method has the disadvantage of being more difficult to calculate than the market price method because it is necessary to segregate the unique costs of all products. In addition, it is not so well known as the market price method but, nevertheless, under many situations only the modified market price method will produce completely satisfactory results.

CHAPTER FIVE

Direct and Absorption Cost Accounting

Full unit costs must be calculated assuming some specific volume of production because unit costs are different at different volumes. Fixed costs are defined as those costs that are fixed in total amount. This means, however, that fixed costs *per unit will vary*. For example, automobile insurance may be $100 a year and is a fixed cost. The cost of automobile insurance per mile, however, will vary with the number of miles driven. If 10,000 miles are driven in a year, insurance will cost 1 cent a mile. If 20,000 miles are driven, insurance will cost only ½ cent a mile. The volume to be used in cost accounting is an important consideration because it can have a significant effect on the unit costs.

Some accountants avoid the problem of volume by using a direct costing system (described next). This does not *solve* the problem because full costs are required for certain management decisions under a direct costing system.

Because the problems of direct costing and volume are related, they are both discussed in this chapter. The first part of the chapter deals with direct costing; the second part deals with the volume to be used in calculating unit costs.

58

DIRECT COSTING

Direct costing is the term applied to a cost accounting system that assigns only the *variable manufacturing costs* to the product. *Absorption costing* is the term applied to a cost accounting system that assigns *all manufacturing costs* to the product. Absorption costing is the traditional system and the type usually described in most cost accounting textbooks. Although direct costing systems were in effect before 1930, it is only since World War II that much interest has been taken in direct costing. During the last decade or so, there have been literally hundreds of articles published on direct costing—some in favor and some against. Within the past several years, many large firms in the United States have changed over to direct costing systems.

Direct Costing Defined

There is some confusion as to the precise definition of a direct costing system. In this book, the term direct costing will be applied to a cost accounting system that treats only variable manufacturing expense as a product cost on the books of account and, consequently, treats fixed and nonvariable manuacturing expense as a period charge to be written off each month. In other words, a direct costing system will segregate variable and fixed manufacturing costs on the books of account.

One of the major problems in establishing a direct costing system is to separate the variable from the fixed costs. (One of the reasons frequently given for not adopting a direct costing system is the difficulty in even defining a variable cost.) Material and direct labor are variable (although there can be exceptions) and present no serious problem. Overhead, however, contains both fixed and variable costs and the separation of these does present a problem. The following methods can be used to separate fixed from variable overhead:

1. Treat overhead as 100 per cent fixed and include only material and labor in product cost.
2. Include as variable cost only those overhead expense categories that are nearly all variable; treat all other overhead expense as fixed.
3. Include as variable cost those overhead expense categories that appear to be 50 per cent more variable; treat all other expenses as fixed.
4. Include as fixed expenses only those expense categories that are nearly all fixed; treat all other expenses as variable.

5. Divide all overhead expenses into variable, semivariable and fixed. Break out the fixed and variable element in each semivariable account. (Several methods for doing this are described in Chapter 6.)

The decision as to which method to use can only be made within the context of a given situation. Other things being equal, the most accurate estimate of variable cost should be used. This is usually method 5. But since method 5 also requires the most work, the added expense may not be justified. Even the most painstaking mathematical analysis to separate the fixed from the variable costs will be only an approximation because the variable cost line is a linear approximation of what almost never is a linear function. (This is explained in more detail in Chapter 6.) The further the actual volume varies from standard, the greater will be the probable error. In certain circumstances, therefore, it may not be worth the expense to use method 5. Method 1 is usually best when overhead represents a relatively small proportion of manufacturing costs and, in general, does not vary much with the level of production. This frequently occurs, for example, in small plants that assemble manufactured components into a finished product.

The decision as to which method to use is determined by: (a) the degree of accuracy required, (b) the cost of separating the fixed from the variable elements in the semivariable costs, and (c) the nature of the overhead costs (in particular, the relative size and the degree of variability). A less accurate method should not be picked for any reason other than economy. For example, method 4 should not be used just to make sure that contribution is not overstated. To understate contribution deliberately by overstating variable costs can lead to faulty management decisions.

Arguments For and Against Direct Costing

The literature on direct costing contains two areas of confusion that occur with considerable regularity. It would be well, therefore, to clarify these areas before proceeding with a discussion of the advantages and disadvantages of a direct costing system.

TWO AREAS OF CONFUSION

The first area of confusion evidently results from a failure to realize that a direct costing system separates fixed from variable costs on the *books of account*. The lack of a direct costing system does not mean that management cannot have variable cost and contribution information;

it means that this information does not come directly from the accounting system but will have to be obtained analytically. (Financial information obtained outside of the books of account is usually called "statistical" data.) Conversely, a direct costing system does not mean that management will be deprived of full cost information; it means that the books of account do not produce this information directly. Arguments for or against direct costing, therefore, that cite the need of management for either variable costs or full costs are not valid.

The second area of confusion results from the public accountants' examinations of the theory behind direct costing. Accountants have tried to show that direct costing is, per se, good or bad. For example, there are accountants who argue that fixed costs are required if goods are to be produced; therefore, these costs are essential to production and should be included in product cost. Because direct costing affects inventory values that must be certified by the public accountant, it is necessary that he examine the theory behind direct costing. In cost accounting, however, the overriding consideration is to provide management with the best information for making decisions. Generally accepted accounting principles are followed only if they help to do this. If a direct costing system provides better information, it should be employed; if it does not, it should not be used.

Because no accounting system (including direct costing) will be the best for all situations, the question to be answered is not "Is direct costing or absorption costing right?" but "Is direct costing better in a particular situation to some alternative costing technique?" Many companies in which direct costing systems have replaced full absorption systems are operating effectively and satisfactorily. It does not appear that anyone can state categorically, therefore, that direct costing systems should not be used. Conversely, there are still many full absorption systems where it is doubtful that a change to direct costing would be an improvement. Consequently, how can full absorption systems be condemned in total?

In most information systems, management will need both total unit cost and variable cost. The decision to adopt a direct cost system should be made because of the advantages of having variable costs rather than the full costs generated by the accounting system.

ADVANTAGES OF DIRECT COSTING

1. *Eliminates profit fluctuations caused by differences between sales and production volume.* The major advantage of a direct costing system to many managers and controllers is that it eliminates fluctuations in profits resulting from differences between the volume of sales and the

volume of production within an accounting period. Management tends to think of profits directly related to the volume of sales. It is, therefore, frequently confusing to management when this month's sales are higher than last month's and yet profits are lower because of underabsorbed overhead.

It often is very difficult for the controller to explain this situation to the nonaccounting-oriented manager. This problem is accentuated when profit-volume (or break even) charts are used extensively. These charts are based on sales revenues and variable costs (see Chapter 9); consequently they do not provide for differences between sales volumes and production volumes. Over- or underabsorbed overhead, therefore, can create a deviation from the profit volume line and, if significant, will tend to limit the value of the profit-volume chart. It is disconcerting to management to see that on the chart profit is right on the line, but to find out later that the satisfactory performance resulted when the overabsorbed overhead offset a poor cost performance.

In evaluating any particular system, the applicability of this advantage will depend principally on the extent to which production volume differs from sales volume during the period covered by the internal profit statement. The existence of over- or underabsorbed overhead, in itself, does not cause profit fluctuations. These fluctuations are caused by differences between sales volumes and production volumes. If sales and production volumes are identical, the profits under full absorption accounting will be the same as the profits under direct costing, even though the financial statements under the former system show a large under- or overabsorbed overhead amount. This can be demonstrated by the following example:

Standard volume	100,000 units
Selling price	$2.50 per unit
Standard variable costs at standard volume	$100,000
Standard fixed manufacturing cost	$100,000
Standard variable cost per unit	$1.00
Standard total cost per unit	$2.00
Actual Sales:	
Situation 1	120,000 units
Situation 2	60,000 units
Situation 3	120,000 units
Actual Production:	
Situation 1	120,000 units
Situation 2	60,000 units
Situation 3	60,000 units
Actual costs equal standard costs in all situations.	

The profits using a direct costing system and an absorption costing system, under each of the three situations, are as follows:

Situation 1

	Using Direct Costing	Using Absorption Costing
Sales	$300,000	$300,000
Standard Cost of Sales	120,000	240,000
Gross Profit	180,000	60,000
Fixed Costs	100,000	—
Overabsorbed Overhead	—	20,000
Net Profit	$80,000	$80,000

Situation 2

Sales	$150,000	$150,000
Standard Cost of Sales	60,000	120,000
Gross Profit	90,000	30,000
Fixed Costs	100,000	—
Underabsorbed Overhead	—	(40,000)
Net (Loss)	$(10,000)	$(10,000)

Situation 3

Sales	$300,000	$300,000
Cost of Sales	120,000	240,000
Gross Profit	180,000	60,000
Fixed Costs	100,000	—
Underabsorbed Overhead	—	(40,000)
Net Profit	$80,000	$20,000

Although the example is extreme, it demonstrates the possible differences in profits between the two methods. It may be argued, of course, that the full absorption system is better because it brings management's attention forcibly to the fact that production levels are low. If this is the information required by the management of a company, then full absorption should be used. (On the other hand, it can also be argued that high production volumes can partially offset the profit effect of unfavorable sales volume.)

Variances between sales and production volumes are generally related to the time period involved. The longer the time period, the closer the two volumes are likely to be. For this reason, monthly profits will usually be much more affected than annual profits.

2. *Product costs approximate differential costs.* A second advantage of direct costing is that the product costs generated through the accounting system tend to approximate differential costs. This helps to eliminate confusion when the accounting costs differ from those used in making product decisions. (Differential costs are explained more fully in Chapter 9. Essentially a differential cost is the amount of cost change resulting from a change in product design or production volume. For short-run changes, differential costs will tend to equal the variable costs as calculated in a direct costing system.)

For example, a study showed that a product could be modified to make it more acceptable to the customer for an increase in costs of $.50 in direct labor and $.50 in variable overhead. Under a full absorption system, this cost increase might show up on the books as $1.50 if the burden rate were 200 per cent. To be sure, the burden on other products would be reduced so that the over-all costs were the same as stated in the study. The fact remains, however, that under a full absorption system, the accounting figures will not reflect this fact. The same conditions will be true when adding a new product to the line or substituting a new product for an old one.

Whether this advantage applies in any particular company will depend on the nature of the business and, again, on how well management understands the system. In a business that characteristically makes frequent changes in design or product mix to gain short-run market advantages, direct costing will usually provide the best monthly accounting information.

A word of caution is in order here. In some cases, product design or mix changes may be infrequent and, when made, may be expected to continue for a period of years. In this case, total costs may be closer than variable costs to the differential costs of the decision. The longer the period of time involved, the closer will be differential and total costs. (Remember: in the long run, all costs are variable.)

3. *Less allocations are required.* A third advantage of a direct costing system is that less allocations are required. For example, it is not necessary to allocate fixed costs to department and product. This not only saves money (in some cost systems, these allocations are made each month) but also eliminates some of the distortions mentioned in Chapter 3 (that is, different costs because products were made on machines purchased at different times). This advantage will apply to companies that do not need to know total unit costs or to have product line profits beyond the contribution amount. This situation is unusual, however, and the question becomes: "Is there an advantage to allocating fixed costs to products outside the books of account?" (Remember, when management needs an

approximation of total costs, it must be done *outside* of the accounting system when direct costing is used.)

ℕ In many cases there is an advantage to allocating fixed costs to products outside of the books of account. The fixed part of product cost is, at best, only a rough approximation and can be used only as a general guide for management action. Running these allocations through the books of account makes them no more accurate and sometimes gives an unwarranted appearance of precision. When fixed costs are allocated to products outside of the books of account, there is often greater flexibility. For example, there is no problem in crossing departmental lines. In the case where one department has prewar equipment and another department has postwar equipment, it is possible to average the total fixed costs of both departments and assign an average amount per unit to each product produced (assuming the products require comparable manufacturing processes).

Once fixed costs have been allocated to product line, it will usually be unnecessary to change more than once a year (and frequently not this often). Fixed costs, by definition, should not change much from month to month and accounting for minor monthly fluctuations will not add accuracy to figures that are already rough approximations.

Whether this advantage applies to any particular company depends upon what the fixed part of the product cost is used for, how involved the calculation is, and whether there are distortions in product cost because of differences in equipment values among departments. In many cases, where the allocation procedure is inexpensive and where there is no distortion in product costs, advantage 3 will not be a valid reason for changing to direct costing.

4. *Contribution is reflected on the books of account.* A fourth advantage that is frequently cited for direct costing is that contribution is reflected in the books of account. Management must know contribution to make many product decisions; if it is not calculated on the books of account, it will have to be done outside of the accounting system. The only question here is "What is the advantage of having contribution reflected in the books of account?" Since management will be provided with the contribution amount involved in any product decision, the principal difference between a full absorption system and a direct costing system is the profit breakdown on the monthly or quarterly financial statements. Under direct costing, management will be shown monthly contribution; under a full absorption system, management will see only gross profit. In any particular system, this advantage will apply only if there appears to be any reason for showing management the contribution amounts on the monthly (or quarterly) profit statements.

5. *Provides better control over fixed costs.* A final advantage proposed by direct costing advocates is that it provides better control over fixed costs. The argument is that fixed costs can be controlled better in total and that direct costing treats fixed costs in total. The control of fixed costs does not appear to be a compelling reason for adopting direct costing. These costs can be controlled in total under either a full absorption or a direct costing system. The only advantage of a direct costing system is that fixed costs are shown in one place, in total, on the monthly income statement. Under a budgetary control system, however, management can compare actual fixed cost in total to budget, even though these figures will not appear on the income statement. If there is no budgetary control system in a company, there may be some advantage to showing fixed costs in total on the income statement. Again, whether this advantage will apply depends on the nature of the business and the cost control system in operation. (If fixed costs were essentially uncontrollable from month to month, for example, there is little advantage to showing them separately.)

DISADVANTAGES OF DIRECT COSTING

Under certain conditions, some of the advantages listed in the previous section can be considered disadvantages. If, for example, the management of a company were prone to make all decisions, both short- and long-term, on the basis of contribution, it might be a disadvantage to have the monthly accounting statements reflect contribution. In addition to these disadvantages that may apply in particular cases, there are five disadvantages to direct costing.

1. *Internal financial statements differ from published reports.* The first disadvantage is that the internal financial statements will differ from the published reports. This results because most direct costing methods are not considered acceptable by the public accounting profession for external financial statements. (Also, most of these methods are not considered acceptable by the Internal Revenue Service for income tax purposes.) Consequently, when a company uses direct costing, it is necessary to increase the value of the inventory to reflect full accounted costs. This adjustment may cause confusion because the internal profit figure will be different from that included in the annual report.

The seriousness of this disadvantage depends on the ability of management to understand the situation. If management understands and agrees that a direct costing system is more useful, there should be little problem. If, however, management is not able (or willing) to understand why internal and external statements are different, this factor could be an important consideration in deciding whether to adopt a direct costing system.

The calculation to adjust the inventories to full cost is usually not an involved problem, with respect to either the public accountant or the Internal Revenue Service. Acceptable methods are available that can be applied to the entire inventory value so that it is not necessary to recalculate the cost of each item. The clerical cost of making this calculation is relatively small.

2. *Monthly profits tend to fluctuate more widely.* The second disadvantage of direct costing is that monthly profits will tend to fluctuate widely where the demand is seasonal. Under a full absorption system, if production is relatively constant, the effects of seasonal changes in sales will be considerably mitigated. With direct costing, however, the same amount of fixed costs will be reflected in the income statement each month regardless of the sales volume; therefore, profits will be higher in above-average months and lower in below-average months.

The seriousness of this disadvantage will depend upon several things: first, upon whether seasonal demand exists; second, if it does exist, upon whether production is more constant than sales (if it is not, the monthly profit fluctuations will not be mitigated); third, upon whether management understands the limitations of the monthly profit estimates. As in the other situations, this disadvantage can only be evaluated within the context of the company that is considering the adoption of a direct costing system.

3. *Direct costing requires a change in the present system.* The third disadvantage of direct costing is that for most companies it entails a departure from accounting methods that have been in effect for some period of time. Any change causes a certain amount of trouble and confusion. A change to a direct costing system, therefore, should not be made unless there are positive advantages for doing so. A company should not change its internal accounting system simply because "it appears to be the thing to do." Direct costing (or any other costing) is not a panacea for management ills. A direct costing system may aid management to make better decisions but it will not compensate for inadequate management.

4. *It is difficult to calculate variable costs.* The fourth disadvantage, offered by proponents of absorption costing, is the inability of some companies to calculate variable costs, or even to agree on a definition. Management must make decisions based on differential costs and, consequently, these costs must be estimated. No matter how inexact the estimate, it is generally better than no estimate at all. The objection refers to having these variable costs reflected on the books of account. Since

the variability of costs will differ under different circumstances, the usefulness of a single calculation of the variability of overhead costs is questioned. The answer to this question must also be decided in the context of a specific situation. If management must make many decisions where variable costs may vary widely, a separate study will be required for each decision. Under these circumstances, little would be gained in having a single, arbitrarily defined variable cost reflected on the books of account. If, however, the variability of overhead costs does not differ much for different types of decisions, the fourth objection to direct costing is not valid.

    5. *Inventories are undervalued.* The fifth disadvantage of direct costing is that inventories are undervalued. There is no question that inventories will have a lower value under a direct costing system than under a full absorption system and, in this respect, could be considered undervalued. Whether this disadvantage applies to any situation will depend on what effect this lower inventory value has. (The same disadvantage applies to the LIFO method of inventory valuation.) To the extent that in direct costing inventories are smaller than in full absorption costing, internal statements will show a lower profit (in the year of the change-over) and lower earned surplus. Since external statements, however, will not be changed, the ability to borrow money or pay dividends will be unaffected. If there are positive reasons for adopting a direct costing system, it is questionable whether lower inventory value is really a disadvantage.

SUMMARY

    The question to be answered with respect to direct costing is *not* whether direct costing is better than full absorption costing. The question *is* whether direct costing is better in a particular situation. The way to decide whether to adopt a direct costing system is to study the advantages and disadvantages that will apply to each specific case. If the advantages do not outweigh the disadvantages, direct costing should not be adopted. For cost accounting purposes, the advantages and disadvantages are those related to the value of the information that management will receive rather than those applicable to theoretical accounting principles.

COST ACCOUNTING VOLUME

    At the beginning of the chapter we stated that it is necessary to have a volume of production in order to calculate unit costs. Variable costs, by definition, are the same at any volume. Fixed costs, on the other hand, are fixed in total and will vary with the volume of production. Consequently, unit costs can only be expressed in terms of dollars per unit at some specific volume. The idea of unit costs being related to volume is quite elementary. It is surprising, however, how many executives accept unit costs as absolute without considering the volume upon which they are based, yet the decision of what volume to use to calculate units costs can frequently have a greater impact on the results than any other decision on cost accounting techniques.

The volumes used by cost accountants to calculate unit costs can be classified into four general types: actual, forecast, capacity, and standard; each is described in detail below.

Before discussing each type and its advantages and disadvantages, it may be well to consider a generalized solution to the problem of volume: *The volume to be used is the one that will result in the best information to management in the specific situation.* The corollary to this generalization is that no one of the four types of volume will be right under every circumstance; it depends what information management needs. The question, therefore, is not whether standard volume is superior to actual volume but whether standard volume is superior to actual volume *in a given situation.*

Actual Volume

As the name implies, the actual volume method means that unit costs are calculated using the actual volume of production for the period. The usual method is to divide the total actual departmental overhead by the total actual departmental direct labor to obtain an overhead rate. This overhead rate is then applied to the actual unit direct labor for each department to obtain the overhead cost per unit. (Obviously, the actual volume method can only be used with an actual cost system; it is not adaptable to a standard cost system.) Actual volume was probably the first volume to be used in cost accounting. It is still today the choice of many cost accountants and managers on the ground that it is the only volume that provides "actual" costs.

The fallacy of this position has been pointed out in several places in this book. There is no absolute "actual" unit cost. This is not a sufficient reason, therefore, for preferring one method over another. There must be a positive benefit in better information before one method can be said to be better (which really means "more useful") than another. The use of actual volume is quite limited because unit costs will be low in periods of high volume and high in periods of low volume; this makes it difficult for management to use unit costs. Only in the most unusual circumstances could costs that fluctuate with volume be used as a guide for pricing action or other revenue decisions. The use of unit costs for even the most primitive cost control is impaired by the fact that changes in volume affect these costs. It is nearly impossible to compare the unit costs of one period with those of another and make any sensible evaluation of the changes. Even costs for inventory valuation can be badly distorted. When volume is low, costs can be seriously overstated and vice versa.

Another disadvantage is that unit costs cannot be calculated until after the end of the period. This can be a disadvantage when customers are charged on a basis of the actual work performed. It is not possible to bill them until after the books are closed. Furthermore, when billing is based on actual costs, it is difficult to explain that volume is the reason for the same job costing a different amount in two different periods.

About the only time that unit costs based on actual volume appear to be useful is when capacity has been set aside for only one purchaser. The less that this capacity is utilized, the more each unit will cost the buyer. This may exist in certain cost plus fixed fee contracts. A company agrees to maintain a facility to supply whatever is demanded by the purchaser. The purchaser agrees to pay the actual cost of the products produced. The less the purchaser demands, the more it will cost him per unit under this kind of agreement. (Even then, it would probably be better to charge a total fee for the capacity plus a variable cost for the units produced.) Such a contract is unusual in most businesses, occurring only in a few types of government contracts.

As a generalization, there are so few instances where actual volume is the best volume to use that, whenever it is used, the reasons for it should be carefully evaluated. There are many companies today using actual volume in their cost accounting system that would be better served by some other volume.

Annual Forecast

When a company uses a standard overhead rate, it is not possible to use actual volume. An approximation of the actual volume is to forecast the coming year's production volume and to calculate the standard overhead rate at this volume. In theory, an overhead rate based on an annual forecast will have all the disadvantages of a rate based on actual volume, except that costing can be done before the books are closed. In practice, however, the annual forecast is widely used and the unsatisfactory effects associated with actual volume are considerably lessened.

The principal problem with using actual volume is caused by the fluctuations in costs as a result of the fluctuations in volume. Monthly volumes tend to fluctuate relatively more widely than annual volumes, particularly where there is a seasonal trend. The use of an annual volume, therefore, is one factor that tends to lessen the period-to-period fluctuations. (Using actual volume, it is impractical in most cases to use annual volume because this requires waiting until the end of the year before unit costs are calculated.)

Even more important than the time period is the fact that the volumes are forecast. People rarely forecast extreme volume levels, either high or low. Thus, even though the actual volume fluctuates significantly from year to year, costs are calculated at a more constant level. In many cases, forecast volume will be very similar to the standard volume described later.

The use of an annual forecast is generally a much more satisfactory basis for calculating unit costs than actual volume. Nevertheless, it has the same problems created by fluctuations in volume. Unit costs will be high in periods of low volume and low in periods of high volume. This can lead management to take precisely the wrong action if unit costs are used as a basis for establishing prices or influencing product mix. Meaningful comparisons of year-to-year unit costs are also difficult.

The reason that annual forecasts usually prove satisfactory is that the volume tends to be reasonably constant from year to year. Since this is the case, it might be better to recognize this fact and use a volume that is designed to be constant.

Capacity Costing

One of the most confusing controversies in current cost accounting theory relates to capacity costing. It has been my experience that most of this confusion comes from defining "capacity." The word capacity must always be preceded by an adjective describing the kind of capacity that is meant because there are at least two commonly used types of capacity: theoretical and practical. Even when modified by the appropriate adjective, it is important to recognize that there are several ways of calculating what is supposed to be the same kind of capacity.

Not only are there serious problems in defining capacities but, in any complicated production situation, many assumptions must be made that will affect the final figures. Two equally competent men will usually estimate two different capacity figures for the same production facility, even though they agree on the type of capacity they are calculating and the definition of that capacity.

In many of the articles that have been written for or against capacity costing, much of the disagreement occurs because the writers have been referring to different kinds of capacity. One author unwittingly shifted back and forth between two kinds of capacity in the same article.

THEORETICAL CAPACITY

Theoretical capacity is defined as the maximum output of a plant or other production unit. There is usually no allowance for down time due to repairs or any loss in production caused by such factors as inefficient scheduling or off-standard labor performance. There are, however, two important assumptions that can affect the volume significantly: one is the number of shifts per week; the other is the assumptions with respect to product mix. A three-shift, seven-day weekly operation will result in more than four times the capacity of a one shift, five-day operation. Also, the mix of products will affect the machine utilization. An ideal mix may make it possible to keep all machines operating at rated capacity all the time. Anything less than an ideal mix will result in some machines operating at less than their rated capacity. In no complex manufacturing operation is it likely that the total theoretical capacity of the plant will equal the sum of the rated capacities of all of the equipment in the plant. When theoretical capacity is discussed, therefore, the term must be defined precisely.

For purposes of this discussion, theoretical capacity will mean the maximum that a plant can produce during the standard work week, assuming "normal" mix of products, but allowing for no loss from inefficient production procedures or down time for repairs. In other words, this would be the production volume if everything went absolutely right.

One school of thought recommends using theoretical capacity to calculate unit costs. The principal reasons given are:

1. It is a constant volume and will eliminate unit cost fluctuations because of volume changes. (This will generally be true. If capacity is increased, it usually means that an increase in equipment has taken place, thereby increasing fixed costs. Because both the numerator and the denominator will be increased, the overhead rate will tend to remain constant.)

2. Other methods of costing include the cost of idle capacity in the unit cost. Costing at theoretical capacity eliminates the cost of idle capacity and thus values inventories on a conservative basis. (A similar argument is that idle capacity is a "loss" and not a "cost" and should not be included in inventory.)

3. The cost of idle capacity is clearly identified in the underabsorbed burden.

The overriding disadvantage in using theoretical capacity is that the resulting unit costs cannot be used for revenue decisions without adding something for those idle capacity costs that are a necessary part of being in business. Costs calculated at theoretical capacity are unattainable and cannot be used by management to determine the adequacy of the pricing structure, the profitability of the various products, or the desirability to expand or contract any of the product lines.

The decision as to whether to use theoretical capacity as a basis for calculating unit cost depends on the information that management needs. If isolating all costs that result from operations at less than theoretical capacity provides the information that management finds most useful, then theoretical capacity should be used (assuming that management understands the limitations of the resulting unit cost figures). If, however, management needs unit costs as a basis for pricing and product decisions, the use of theoretical capacity will usually not be justified.

PRACTICAL CAPACITY

Practical capacity is also defined in various ways. In most cases, practical capacity allows for necessary down time for repairs and for normal restrictions in available capacity for such factors as line balancing and scheduling. In other words, it represents the possible production that a plant could attain if there were no shortage of orders and if the plant were being operated at normal efficiency. (Notice that there are several areas where individual judgment can affect the figures.) A frequent modification of this definition allows for a margin of capacity to provide for seasonal peaks and normal growth. This means that: (1) it is necessary to maintain some idle capacity to meet seasonal peaks; and (2) some idle capacity is normally expected when a facility is first built to allow for the subsequent growth of sales volume.

THEORETICAL VS. PRACTICAL CAPACITY

Although both theoretical and practical capacity are used in describing "capacity costing," there is a wide difference in these two concepts. At theoretical capacity, unit costs contain no allowance for idle capacity and must be adjusted before these cost figures can be used by management for decisions in the pricing or product areas. On the other hand, unit costs calculated at practical capacity exclude from unit costs only the cost of abnormal idle capacity. (Abnormal idle capacity is that resulting from an insufficient sales volume or an inefficient production performance. This will differ somewhat depending on how practical capacity is defined. The purpose in all cases, however, is to allow for necessary down time in calculating unit costs.) In general, unit costs calculated on the basis of practical capacity are much more useful to management in making pricing and product decisions. They represent more nearly the costs for which the customer should pay. If some idle capacity is required (and it almost always is) as part of an efficient production and marketing plan, it is to be expected that the cost of this idle capacity will be passed on to the customer. Also, unit costs based on practical capacity are much more realistic for forward planning purposes than cost based on theoretical capacity. The latter costs, by definition, are unattainable because theoretical capacity is unattainable.

Even in the area of underabsorbed burden, management will usually receive more useful information from using practical capacity. Because there will always be an underabsorbed burden using theoretical capacity, management cannot use this information for deciding when there is a problem. It is necessary to know what the underabsorbed overhead should be at normal efficiency. When the underabsorbed burden exceeds this amount, management will know that a problem exists. This figure is obtained directly when practical capacity is used. In most businesses, however, this consideration is not important because management does not normally rely on the under- or overabsorbed burden amount as a source of information on production volumes.

There can be no categorical statement that practical capacity is better than theoretical capacity for calculating unit costs. Each method will result in different information; the correct method is the one that provides the most meaningful information to management. Of the two methods, practical capacity will be the more useful method in most business situations. When using theoretical capacity, therefore, the requirements of the particular situation should be analyzed to make sure that the method is justified in terms of more useful information to management.

Standard Volume

Standard volume is usually defined as the average volume expected over the next five to ten years. The General Motors Corporation has used the concept of standard volume as a guide to pricing and product decisions for more than thirty years. Albert Bradley's description of the concept of standard volume and its use as a guide to management in making pricing decisions is still a classic in the field.[1]

The principal purpose of standard volume is for facility planning. It is used only incidentally for calculating unit costs. The usual method is to determine how much practical capacity is required to meet standard volume, taking into account seasonal fluctuations, cyclincal fluctuations and secular growth. Plants are then built to provide this capacity. For example, in the early postwar years, General Motors estimated that prac-

[1] N.A.C.A. *Bulletin,* January 1927.

tical capacity would have to equal 125 per cent of standard volume. The excess capacity was necessary to meet peak sales requirements.

Which Volume to Use?

In cases where a company has established a standard volume and built facilities in line with this volume, standard volume is the most useful for calculating unit costs. When a company does not have a formal standard volume, should it establish such a volume for calculating unit costs?

In most business situations, the best volume for calculating unit costs requires two conditions: (1) the volume represents a realistic average expected volume of sales; and (2) practical capacity is (or will be) consistent with this volume. In other words, the facilities should be such that practical capacity is in line with standard volume. Under this condition, no problem exists in deciding which volume to use. Where the two differ, there are three possible actions:

1. Use standard volume. This could have the disadvantage of either overstating unit costs (if excess capacity exists) or understating them (if there is insufficient capacity).
2. Use practical capacity. This could have the disadvantage of distorting unit costs if the capacity was significantly different from the standard volume. For instance, if practical capacity is 100,000 units a year, with fixed costs equal to $100,000 annually, but if the expected sales volume is only 50,000 units, there is a large amount of excess capacity which should not be reflected in the unit costs. If unit costs are calculated at practical capacity, the fixed cost per unit will be $1.00. If, however, the capacity was in line with the expected sales, a plant with an annual practical capacity of 50,000 units might reflect entirely different fixed costs. Fixed costs for a plant to produce 50,000 units might equal $75,000 annually, for a unit fixed cost of $1.50.
3. Use standard volume but eliminate the cost of idle capacity from the product cost (or add costs if the capacity is inadequate). This means that fixed costs will be adjusted to reflect the amount that would have been incurred if practical capacity were in line with standard volume.

Of the three courses of action, the third is the most accurate. In most cases, however, the distortion in unit costs may not be large enough to warrant the extra work involved. In addition, the theoretical justification for eliminating the costs of excess capacity (or, worse, adding fixed costs that do not exist) are usually difficult to explain to management.

SUMMARY

Because the volume that is used in calculating unit costs can have a significant effect on the absolute amount of the cost, it is an important consideration in any cost accounting system. The volume to be used is dependent upon the use to which the cost figures are to be put. If, these unit costs are to be used principally to guide management in pricing and product decisions, the volumes in order of preference are as follows:

1. Standard volume when the practical capacity of the facilities is approximately in line with this volume.
2. Standard volume with fixed costs adjusted to reflect what they would be if capacity were in line with standard volume.
3. Practical capacity if there is no standard volume.
4. Standard volume when capacity figures are not available.

The objectives are to: (1) use a volume that will be reasonably constant (or have constant relationship to capacity) so that costs between periods will not be affected by random changes in the level of production; (2) exclude from unit cost the cost of excess capacity that results from inefficiency, poor planning, or lower than projected sales volume; (3) include in unit cost the cost of capacity required to meet normal down time, product mix, seasonal fluctuations and secular growth.

In some cases, it may be necessary to use annual sales estimates. When a company has many products and changing conditions (such as a rapid growth), estimating either standard volume or capacity may be impractical because both are changing each year. In cases such as this, annual sales estimates provide the best volume.

VOLUME AND DIRECT COSTING

The use of direct costing has been recommended as a means of eliminating the problem of volume. Direct costing affects only variable costs and no volume assumptions are necessary because, by definition, these costs are the same per unit at all volumes. It is true that the use of direct costing will eliminate the problem on the books of account. If management needs total unit cost figures (and it usually does), it will still be necessary to decide on a volume in order to make these calculations, even though they are made outside of the books of account. If management does not need total unit costs, there is no problem with respect to volume in any case. Direct costing, therefore, is only a solution to this problem when total costs are not required but, because of full absorption accounting, a volume is needed. In this case, it is only a matter of adapting the cost accounting system to the requirements of management; this action should have been taken under any circumstances.

CHAPTER SIX

Budgetary Control (Part I)

GENERAL

A budget serves two purposes: planning and control. First, the budget when approved by management becomes the basis for planning and coordinating the activities of the company. For example, the sales budget becomes the basis for planning the future requirements for material and personnel. The profit budget and the capital budget are used to plan future cash requirements. Second, the budget is used as a means of control. Control is exercised by comparing actual performance with the budget and taking appropriate action when they differ.

Many types of budgets are in use today in business. There are expense budgets which cover all or part of the costs of operating a business. When the expense budget is broadened to include revenue, it becomes a profit budget. The profit budget is used to plan annual profits and, subsequently, to control actual profit performance. In addition, there are financial budgets that are principally concerned with cash planning, and there are capital budgets that are concerned with expenditures for fixed assets. Only expense budgets and profit budgets will be considered here. Capital budgets, financial budgets, and long-range profit plans (also a type of budget) are outside the scope of this book. Also, because the book is principally concerned with cost control, the control aspect of budgeting will be emphasized.

Operating and Programmed Budgets

For budgetary control purposes, it is necessary to separate expense budgets into two types—operating and programmed—because each type uses a different method of control and, consequently, is treated differently by management.

Operating budgets cover those expenses for which it is practicable to establish a standard of efficiency. These will be mainly material, direct labor and manufacturing overhead. In some cases, however, parts of other types of costs are covered by operating budgets. For example, under administrative expense, the payroll or collection of accounts receivable might be controlled by an operating budget; or, in merchandising, the shipping department expense might be controlled by an operating budget. The method of controlling costs in an operating budget is to establish an efficient cost standard and to measure subsequently actual performance against this standard. Cost control is achieved by *motivation* and *evaluation*. By reporting actual expenditures against an objective amount, line management is motivated to produce as efficiently as possible. The budget performance report gives top management a basis for *evaluating* the effectiveness of line management in controlling costs. Cost control is achieved by promoting the efficient and replacing the inefficient. The principal *problem* in an operating budget is to decide how much each job should cost, that is, establishing effective cost standards.

Programmed budgets cover those expenses that are subject to management's discretion within a reasonable degree. They cover mainly research and development costs, merchandising expense and administrative expense. A programmed budget provides cost control by allowing management to *participate in the planning* of the programmed expenditures. In reviewing programmed budgets, management does not usually concern itself with setting standards of gauging efficiency. The cost control is exercised exclusively by deciding the size of the task to be undertaken. For example, in approving a research and development budget, management will control expenses by deciding which research projects should be undertaken and how much to spend on each. Costs will not be controlled by trying to establish some kind of objective cost standards for the department. For this reason, the budget performance reports in programmed budgets are not a basis for evaluating an executive on his ability to produce efficiently. The principal *problem* in a programmed budget is to decide the magnitude of the job to be performed.

It is important that the two types of budgets be clearly distinguished throughout the entire budgetary control system. Each type presents a different problem to management and it is important for management to recognize this. For example, the author has seen confusion arise from management's trying to make a decision with respect to the level of efficiency represented in a proposed engineering budget. Management attention was directed to the impossible task of attempting to decide whether the budget represented an efficient level of performance; the real task of deciding whether the projects that were proposed were in accordance with management's thinking was largely ignored.

Some cost items contain elements of both operating and programmed expenses. A merchandising budget, for example, may have an operating budget to cover warehousing expense and a programmed budget to cover advertising, sales staff, and the other merchandising costs. (This type of budget is discussed in Chapter 7.)

Budgeting for Material and Direct Labor

Included in operating expenses are direct material, direct labor, manufacturing overhead, some parts of merchandising expense (such as warehousing costs), and occasionally, certain research and administrative expenses.

When a standard cost system is in effect, the budget for direct material and direct labor is the same as the standard cost. When a standard cost system is not in effect, the problem of establishing budgets for these two items of expense is the same as the problem of setting cost standards. The material budget is based, insofar as possible, on engineering specifications and projected price levels; the labor budget is based, insofar as possible, on time study standards. The actual expenses are compared to budget and the variance analyzed in some meaningful manner, as described in Chapter 2.

Occasionally, a question is raised as to the difference between a standard cost and a budget with respect to direct material and direct labor. The answer is that, in most cases, there is none. Sometimes these costs are called budgeted costs when standard costs are not reflected on the books of account. For example, a company maintains an actual cost system but compares the actual costs to the budget or standard *outside of the books of account.* This is just a matter of accounting procedure; the net results from management's point of view are exactly the same as if the standard costs had been carried through the books.

In summary, then, in most instances the standard cost for material and labor will be the budgeted cost. If a standard cost system exists, therefore, there is no additional problem created by a budgetary control system. When a standard cost system does not exist, the problems of establishing budgets are the same as those for setting cost standards. The budgetary reports for these expenses will be similar to the variance analyses described in Chapter 2. It is only in unusual circumstances that the standard costs and the budgeted costs for these two expenses are different.

MANUFACTURING OVERHEAD BUDGETS

In the area of manufacturing overhead expense, the problems of budgeting differ from those of establishing cost standards. Establishing an overhead budget is more complex and more difficult than establishing material or direct labor budgets because manufacturing overhead is not generally subject to precise engineering analyses.

When a company has both a standard cost system and a manufacturing overhead budget, the budgeted costs at standard volume are the basis for the standard overhead cost. When a company has only a standard cost system, the standard overhead costs are usually based on the historical relationship between the direct labor and the overhead expense. Establishing an effective overhead budget, however, is usually much more complex than simply examining the historic relationship between overhead and direct labor. Furthermore, the reporting of actual performance against budge is usually undertaken in considerably greater detail than the traditional standard cost variance analysis. In general, therefore, a standard cost system, without an overhead budget, provides only loose control over overhead expense.

An effective overhead budgetary control system will provide an efficient cost standard for overhead expenditures and then measure the actual performance against this standard. As stated previously, the existence of such a standard, together with appropriate performance reports, will motivate the foreman or plant manager to try to attain or better this standard; the performance against these standards will provide management with a basis for evaluating his cost performance.

There are three major areas in an effective overhead budgetary control system:

1. Establishing a relationship between manufacturing overhead costs and the volume of production so that the budget authorization will reflect the amount that should be spent at actual volume;

2. Administrating the budget, particularly establishing efficient overhead cost standards; and

3. Establishing an effective reporting system.

Each of these areas is discussed below.

Cost-Volume Relationship

The problem with respect to the volume of operations occurs because manufacturing overhead costs are partly variable and partly fixed. If the overhead budget is established on a dollar-per-unit basis (as standard costs are), standard volume is the only volume where a fair authorization is provided. For example:

Standard Volume .... 100,000 units
Variable Overhead Costs $200,000
Fixed Overhead Costs $100,000
  Total Budgeted Overhead $300,000

$$\text{Standard Overhead Cost Per Unit} = \frac{\$300,000}{100,000} \text{ or } \$3.00 \text{ per unit.}$$

If the overhead authorization were based on $3.00 per unit, at 80,000 units of production the overhead authorization would be 80,000 × $3, or $240,000. If, however, the department was operating at budgeted efficiency, the actual costs would be $100,000 (fixed expense) + $2.00 (variable cost per unit) × 80,000, or $260,000. The budget performance report would show that the department had spent $20,000 *more than budget,* even though the level of efficiency was exactly at budgeted levels. The reason for this, of course, is that $100,000 of overhead cost is fixed at any volume. It is clearly more appropriate to have a budget allowance based on the fixed cost plus the variable cost per unit multiplied by the units produced. Budgets employing this principle are known as flexible or variable budgets. Graphically, this can be shown as follows:

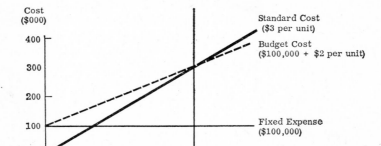

MANUFACTURING OVERHEAD EXPENSE

The budgeted line provides the authorization at any volume. The lower the volume, the less the authorization but only by the amount of the variable cost. In this way, the budget authorization is adjusted to the amount that *should* have been spent at the actual volume of production; the difference between actual and budget is the result of efficiency or inefficiency.

THE FLEXIBLE BUDGET EQUATION

The standard technique for budget authorization under a flexible budget system is expressed by the equation for a straight line, as follows:

$y = a + bx$, where
$y =$ the total budget authorization at volume x,
$a =$ total fixed costs,
$b =$ variable cost per unit,
$x =$ volume in units.

Although the mathematics of authorizing budget expenditures on a fixed and variable basis are quite straightforward, few overhead expenses will vary with volume on a straight-line basis in actual business situations. The rate of variability of these expenses will be different at different volumes. For example, the rate of scrap expense often tends to increase as volume increases. At 80 per cent of standard volume, the scrap rate may be one bad item in 100; at 130 per cent of standard volume it may be three bad items in 100. Conversely, some expenses tend to level off at higher volumes. The increase in indirect labor between 80 per cent and 100 per cent of standard volume may be greater than the increase between 100 per cent and 120 per cent. Another complication in many production processes is that some expenses tend to increase in steps. For example, it may be necessary to add one foreman with each 10 per cent change from standard volume. Between 100 per cent and 109 per cent of standard volume, therefore, no increase in the cost of indirect labor will occur, but at 110 per cent of standard volume, it is necessary to add one man. In summary, then, manufacturing overhead expense, as experienced in most industries, does not fit into a simple, straight-line mathematical function. It is important to remember this when analyzing budget performance. The best that can be done is to *approximate a linear relationship between cost and volume over a limited range of volume.*

SEPARATING FIXED AND VARIABLE MANUFACTURING OVERHEAD

The *first step* in establishing a flexible budget is to subdivide all manufacturing overhead accounts into fixed, variable and semivariable.

This is done analytically by examining each expense to see which it should be. For example, depreciation, property taxes, property insurance, building maintenance, and the plant manager's office are generally considered completely fixed whereas supplies are usually considered completely variable. (In general, only a small number of overhead accounts are completely variable.)

The *second step* is to examine each of the semivariable accounts to see whether the fixed and variable portion of any of these can be separated by inspection. For example, the demand charge for power may be treated as fixed and the remainder of power expense as variable. Or, the estimated cost of heating the building may be treated as fixed and the other steam costs treated as variable. In making this analysis, it is unnecessary to establish exact relationships between fixed and variable because this is usually not possible. It is sufficient to have approximate relationships. Particularly in accounts with small values, the most practical course is to classify the account as either entirely fixed or entirely variable.

The *third step* is to segregate the fixed and variable elements of those semivariable accounts that cannot be segregated readily by inspection. (These will usually include most of indirect labor, utilities, maintenance expenses, fringe benefits, and scrap and defect costs.) There are several methods for separating the fixed and variable elements in a semivariable cost. Before discussing these methods, however, the measurement of volume must be considered.

MEASUREMENT OF VOLUME

The task of separating the fixed and variable elements of an expense account involves calculating: (1) the fixed expense at zero volume; and (2) the variable cost per unit of volume. If a department manufactured only one product, there would be no problem in expressing the volume— it is in units produced. Since a one-product department is unusual, some other measure of volume must be used. If a department makes only a limited number of comparable products, it is possible to express volume in terms of standard units. For example, if unit A were considered standard, unit B 80 per cent of standard, and unit C 110 per cent of standard, production could be estimated as follows:

	Actual Units Produced	Production in Standard Units
A	100,000	100,000
B	100,000	80,000
C	100,000	110,000
TOTAL	300,000	290,000

In most instances, even this method is not practicable because of the number and diversity of parts produced in the typical department. In these cases it is usual to use direct labor (either dollars or hours) as a measure of volume. In using direct labor, two things should be noted:

1. Standard direct labor should be used. If not, inefficient direct labor can result in excess overhead authorization. (This was explained in Chapter 2.)

2. Because volume is measured in terms of direct labor, it does not follow that direct labor creates the overhead costs. Production creates overhead costs and the direct labor is merely a measure of production.

In the examples used throughout the remainder of this chapter, standard direct labor dollars will be used as a measure of the volume of production.

SEPARATING SEMIVARIABLE EXPENSES INTO FIXED AND VARIABLE COMPONENTS

The methods for separating semivariable expenses into their fixed and variable elements are as follows:

1. Estimate the fixed cost at zero volume and the total cost at standard volume. The slope of the line drawn between these two points represents the variable cost per unit of volume.

For example, the cost of supervision is $200,000 at a standard volume of $1,000,000 standard direct labor; $100,000 of this is considered to be fixed in that this amount of expense will be incurred at zero volume. The variable cost rate would be $\frac{100,000}{1,000,000}$, or 10 per cent. The budget authorization equation would be:

$$y = 100,000 + .10x, \text{ or}$$

Total supervisory cost at any volume (x) will be $100,000 + 10 per cent of standard direct labor at volume x.

This method has the advantage of simplicity. It also has the advantage of having a fixed cost that is meaningful to the operating personnel. (In some of the other methods, the fixed expense is determined by a mathematical equation and is not directly related to expected levels of overhead costs at zero volume.)

The main disadvantage of this method is that the variable expense rate represents the *average* variability over a wide range of volume; whereas, most of the time, the equation will be used to authorize overhead at a volume close to standard. As already explained, most overhead costs are not linear from zero volume to capacity. This means that the degree of variability will be different at different volumes. A more accurate approximation of variability can be obtained by measuring the relationship of costs to volume in the range of expected operations (for example, 80 to 120 per cent of standard volume), rather than in the range of 0 to 100 per cent of standard volume. The limitations of this method are evident from the fact that the variable expense authorization at standard volume is dependent upon the definition of fixed costs at zero volume. One company defines fixed costs as those that would continue through a six months' shutdown. This will result in a different equation than if fixed costs were defined as those that would continue for a week after shutdown. (Both definitions are for fixed costs at zero volume.) Clearly, the definition of fixed costs at zero volume has no effect on the expected variability at standard volume.

2. Another method is to estimate the total cost at two volumes, for example, 80 per cent and 120 per cent of standard volume. A line is drawn through these points and extended to zero volume. The point where this line intercepts the cost line at zero volume (the y-intercept) is the fixed cost. The slope of the line is the variable cost per unit.

For example, assume that standard direct labor is $1,000,000 at standard volume. At 80 per cent of standard volume ($800,000 standard direct labor), it is estimated that supervision should be $450,000. At 120 per cent of standard volume ($1,200,000 standard direct labor), supervision should be $500,000. The variable cost rate is calculated as follows:

	Supervision	Direct Labor
Cost at 120% of SV	$500,000	$1,200,000
Cost at 80% of SV	450,000	800,000
Difference	$50,000	$400,000

Variable cost rate $= \dfrac{50,000}{400,000} = .125$ or 12.5 per cent of standard direct labor dollars.

Fixed cost = Total cost at 80 per cent of standard volume minus variable cost at 80 per cent of standard volume or $450,000 - (800,000 \times .125) = \$350,000$.

(The calculation can also be made using 120 per cent of standard volume.)

The budget equation then is:

$$y = 350,000 + .125x, \text{ or}$$

Budgeted cost at volume x is $350,000 + 12.5 per cent of the standard direct labor cost at volume x.

This equation can also be developed by plotting the two points on a graph and drawing a straight line between them. The fixed cost and variable cost rate can then be read directly from the graph.

This method has the advantage of calculating the rate of variability over the range of volume most likely to occur. It has the disadvantage of having a fixed cost that has been developed mathematically. It will be only a coincidence if this is the cost that would be incurred at zero volume. The fixed cost is merely the extrapolation of the line drawn between the two estimated costs. It is required only for the budget equation and it is not supposed to represent the cost at zero volume. This fact is sometimes difficult for operating personnel to understand and, because they do not understand it, they tend to suspect its accuracy.

It should be noted also that both method 1 and method 2 develop the budget equation by calculating only two points. Any distortion in either of these points can have a significant effect on the resulting equation.

3. A third method is to plot the actual expenses for some previous period and fit a straight line to the points either by inspection or by the method of least squares (see Appendix B). The usual procedure is to use monthly data for the past 12 to 24 months. Frequently, unusual months are either eliminated or adjusted. Also, the periods of either extremely high or low volumes are sometimes excluded.

One advantage of this method is that it provides a measure of the *validity* of the equation. If there is a good linear relationship between the level of costs and the volume, it is immediately evident in the fit of the line. (Usually, visual inspection of the fit is all that is required. It is possible, however, to calculate goodness of fit statistically.) Conversely, if the fit is not good, this is also evident. A second advantage of this method is that the slope of the line is determined by many points instead of just two. The effect of a distortion in any plot point is reduced proportionately to the number of points that have been plotted.

A disadvantage of method 3 is that it provides only historical data with respect to variability of the cost. One of the main advantages of a flexible budgetary control system is that it makes operating supervisors aware of the necessity of reducing costs quickly as volume is reduced. Usually, the adoption of a flexible budget will result in better cost control with resulting lower costs. (If it did not, what would be the point of installing it?) Historical variability, before the installation of a flexible budget, may not represent a desirable relationship between cost level and volume.

Not only may the historical relationship of cost to volume be undesirable but the absolute level of historical overhead cost may not represent an adequate degree of efficiency. These two points should be kept in mind when using this method for calculating the budget equation.

4. There are several other methods that are combinations of these three. For example, some companies estimate the overhead costs at several production volumes and fit a line to the data. This method is very good (although more costly) because it eliminates the danger of basing the equation on only two points.

Another method that is sometimes used is to estimate the variability of each expense from historical data and then develop a total budgeted cost at standard volume. The line is drawn through the total cost at standard volume and extended to zero volume to obtain the fixed expense part of the equation. For example, an historical study of cost levels reveals that supervision expense varies $.05 for every dollar change in standard direct labor, that is, a variable rate of 5 per cent. It is further estimated that at a standard volume (1,000,000 standard direct labor dollars) the supervision expense should be $150,000. At zero volume, the supervision will be 150,000 — ($1,000,000 × .05), or $100,000. The equation, therefore, is $y = 100,000 + .05x$. This equation can be developed from a graph by drawing a line with a slope of .05 for each $1.00 change in standard direct labor through the $150,000 point at standard volume. This line intercepts the y axis at $100,000.

NON-LINEAR METHODS

The flexible budget equation is a linear approximation of what is almost never a linear function. Many overhead costs are curvilinear (that is, the rate of change is different at different volume levels). Other costs change in steps (for example, supervision may change by one foreman with every 10 per cent change in volume). In order to have a budget that will take these conditions into account, some companies employ a step budget. A step budget, as the name implies, is one that is estimated at several volumes, for example, at 60, 70, 80, 90, 100, 110, and 120 per cent of standard volume; the budget, instead of changing linearly with volume, changes in "steps." Each month, the authorized expense is equal to the budgeted amount for the volume that is closest to the actual. If actual volume is 73 per cent of standard, the 70 per cent budget will be used; if actual volume is 97 per cent of standard, the 100 per cent budget will be used. In some systems, the budget authorization will be calculated by interpolating between two steps. For example, if the actual volume is 73 per cent, the authorized budget will be the 70 per cent budget plus 30 per cent of the difference between the 70 per cent budget and the 80 per cent budget.

On the surface, it would appear that step budgets are the solution to the problem of adjusting authorized expense levels to the actual volume of production. Unfortunately, several problems that are associated with the use of the step budget tend to limit its value. These problems account for the fact that the step budget is used relatively infrequently in modern manufacturing plants.

The first problem that is created by the step budget is the cost of estimating and evaluating 7 to 10 or more amounts for each expense. Suppose that a plant has 50 cost centers and 50 semi-variable expense classifications. (This is not an unusually large number.) The typical step budget would require between 17,500 (50 × 50 × 7) and 25,000 (50 × 50 × 10) individual estimates of expense levels. The time and cost of making this many estimates (not to mention evaluating them) can be nearly prohibitive.

The second problem with the step budget is that it does not tie into the rest of the cost accounting system. For example, if direct costing is employed, it is necessary to use a single variable cost per unit. This means that there will be a difference between the standard variable overhead and the budgeted variable overhead. If a full cost system is employed, the analysis of variance becomes much more complicated.

A third problem with a step budget is that many simplifications and approximations that are possible with straight-line equations are not practicable when a step budget is used.

These problems do not mean that a step budget should not be employed. They do mean, however, that the step budget is not the answer to the problem of the cost-volume relationship in most overhead budgets. A step budget, properly prepared, is undoubtedly more accurate than the typical straight-line budget. The question to be answered is whether the increase in accuracy that a step budget provides is worth the problems that such a budget creates.

Several adaptations of step budgets are sometimes used to improve the quality of the flexible budget. Three of these are:

1. The use of a step budget for indirect labor only. This will reduce the cost of preparation, but it still does not avoid the second and third problems described above.

2. The preparation of two or three budgets that cover major changes. For example, a regular flexible budget would be prepared for one-shift operation and another for two-shift operation. (Two budgets will normally be required if the number of shifts changes during the year.)

3. The use of a typical flexible budget for everything but evaluating the foreman. The departmental reports will include certain overhead

costs (such as indirect labor) on a step function. All reports, except the departmental, will be based on straight-line equations. This method has the advantage of correcting the step problem at the departmental level. When all departments are combined, the step differences tend to offset.

In summary, the step budget is more accurate than the flexible budget, but it is more costly to prepare and less adaptable to the typical cost accounting and control system. It should be used where the increase in accuracy is worth accepting the disadvantages. In my experience, non-linear methods are generally more applicable to small plants. In large plants, there are such large numbers of expense items that, although they may change in steps, they change at different volumes and, in total, approximate a linear function. In small plants, however, certain costs are so important that a change can have a significant effect on total costs.

MANUFACTURING EXPENSES THAT DO NOT VARY WITH VOLUME

In some types of businesses, overhead costs will not vary with volume. There are two general causes for this: (1) the nature of the business is such that all overhead is more or less fixed; (2) it is management's policy not to reduce the labor force during slack periods.

The first condition tends to be true in many chemical plants. If the plant is producing at all, it may require the full complement of people. Under these conditions, the overhead will be nearly the same at 60 per cent of standard volume as at 100 per cent. Also, in small companies, manufacturing overhead costs frequently will not vary with volume because the number of indirect labor people are so small that all are needed within fairly wide ranges of production. (In this case, however, budgets are hardly required; control is exercised by personal observation.)

Another instance when overhead will not vary with volume occurs if management is not interested in reducing indirect labor when production falls. (This attitude may not be caused entirely by altruism; good people may leave the company if subjected to frequent layoffs.) In this case, the only advantage of having a flexible budget is that it informs management on a month-to-month basis what the no-layoff policy is costing. If this information is not pertinent, then flexible budgets would not be applicable.

DECIDING WHICH METHOD TO USE

There is no one method for estimating variable expense that is better than the other. As in all cases of cost accounting and budgetary control procedure, the method to be used is the one that best fits the individual circumstance. There are, however, two general rules:

1. Use the simplest method that will give reasonable results; and
2. Wherever possible, use a method that can be easily understood by the line supervisor.

AMOUNT OF DETAIL

So far, only the methods for establishing the variable budget equation have been discussed; nothing has been said about the accounting detail to which these equations should be applied. At one extreme some companies develop a single equation to cover the entire overhead expense. At the other extreme, some companies develop an equation for each account and subaccount in the ledger. (Obviously, somewhere in between is the usual practice.)

The *first step* is to decide the minimum detail required for control. In most cases this would be by department and major expense series. For example, each department (both service and production) would need a separate budget if each department manager was to be responsible for the costs that he incurs. By department, it is usually sufficient to have performance against budget by indirect labor, supplies, utilities, maintenance, scrap, and so forth. In some cases, additional detail on indirect labor performance (for example, supervision, clerks, inspections, setup, and so forth) may be desirable. A separate equation is necessary for every item of expense included on the performance report. For example, a plant with eight departments and 10 classifications of expense that management wishes to have reported will need 80 equations for developing flexible budgets.

Once the minimum detail is established, the next step is to develop the equations by the methods previously described. In developing these equations it may be necessary to go into more detail than is required by management. For example, if management needs information only for indirect labor in total, a single equation could be developed for indirect labor. On the other hand, it may be necessary to develop several equations and add them together. The general rule is to use the minimum detail consistent with reasonable accuracy.

In the previous paragraph, it was stated that the equations could be added. This characteristic of the budget equation makes it possible to to combine or separate any expense grouping within a department. For example, the 10 departmental equations mentioned above can be added into a single equation for each department. A simplified example of this is as follows:

The ABC Factory

Summary of Budget Equations

	Department A	Department B
Indirect Labor	$50,000 + .10x$	$20,000 + .15x$
Supplies	$1,000 + .05x$	$500 + .10x$
Maintenance	$5,000 + .15x$	$10,000 + .20x$
Depreciation	$50,000$	$100,000$
TOTAL	$106,000 + .30x$	$130,500 + .45x$

(x = volume, expressed in standard direct labor dollars.)

The department equations cannot be added together to get a total company equation; neither can expense categories (for example, indirect labor) in all departments be added together to get an equation for the total expense. Only equations that have the same volume base can be added. If the plant produced only one product and the equations were developed on the basis of the number of units produced (x = number of units produced) all equations could be added because they all have the same volume base.

APPLICABILITY OF THE FLEXIBLE BUDGETS TO
AREAS OUTSIDE OF MANUFACTURING COSTS

The question frequently arises as to whether flexible budgetary control techniques can be applied to other areas besides manufacturing overhead costs. (The question comes up most frequently with respect to selling expense, which will be discussed specifically in the next chapter.) The purpose of this section is to provide a guide to answering the more general question of the applicability of flexible budgets to any area of expense control.

The following conditions are required for an effective flexible budgetary control system:

1. There should be a direct relationship between input (cost) and output. No measure of variability is perfect (even direct material is rarely 100 per cent variable). All variable budgets, therefore, provide only approximations of budgeted expense levels. The problem is to decide when the relationship between output and input is sufficiently direct to be usable for budgetary control.

2. There must be a measurable output. This is so obvious that it requires little comment. Administration expenses are examples of costs where the output is usually not measurable.

3. The relationship between input and output should be short-run. Since flexible budgets are used to control monthly costs, the input should have an immediate effect on the output.

4. It should be desirable to minimize the unit input, given a required output. The effect of a flexible budget is to put pressure for cost reductions as volume is reduced. In production, because it is generally desirable to attain the lowest unit costs, the flexible budget provides pressure in the right direction. In advertising, however, this is not true; unit costs tend to increase as the amount of advertising increases because the advertising is being directed at "harder to sell" prospects. Here the objective is not to minimize unit costs but to continue advertising until the cost of the last increment of advertising expense equals the contribution from the resulting incremental sales. For this reason (among others) a flexible budget for advertising costs will not provide a reasonable control.

The test of an effective flexible budgetary control system is whether it motivates people to take the most desirable action. Test this particularly at the extremes to see if people are motivated to take the correct action from the company viewpoint.

OVERHEAD BUDGETS AND DAY-TO-DAY COST CONTROL

It should be noted that an overhead budget system will not normally provide the line supervisor with a tool for controlling his costs on a day-to-day basis. The line supervisor does not wait for the budget report to reduce his labor force when volume drops, to fix a broken steam pipe, or to correct a quality problem. Depending on the size and complexity of the department, day-to-day control is exercised by personal observation and special daily and weekly reports of critical cost items.

The budget is designed to give the plant manager over-all control of manufacturing costs. From the budget he can tell if everything is going well or not. If it has not been going well, he can ascertain whether corrective action has been taken. Subsequently, he can find out whether this action has been effective in correcting the problem.

Administration of Manufacturing Expense Budgets

INTRODUCING A MANUFACTURING EXPENSE BUDGET SYSTEM

The administrative problems of introducing a manufacturing expense budget system are usually far more difficult than the technical problems. The manufacturing expense budget is different from most of the other accounting and control activities in that *it is designed to evaluate operating personnel* from the plant manager down to the foreman. Operating personnel may complain about other accounting activities because too much time is being spent on clerical work. To them the accountants are, at worst, a nuisance and, at best, somewhat of a help. Now introduce the operating budget. These same accounting people are responsible for preparing the monthly "report card" that will tell how well the line supervisor has done. On the basis of this report card, the line supervisor may be promoted, demoted, or even discharged. Is it any wonder that he faces the prospect of the introduction of a budgetary control system with certain misgivings? Many of these qualms may be directed at the accounting personnel who have moved from the position of a nuisance to that of a menace.

From the point of view of the line supervisor, the introduction of budgets can mean:

1. He will be evaluated on his cost performance. Since he is evidently doing all right up to now, he has nothing to gain and everything to lose.

2. He will have to work harder and under more pressure. (Remember that one of the major purposes of the budget is to *motivate* him to greater effort.)

3. If he succeeds in cutting costs under the new budget system, it could be construed that he was working inefficiently before its introduction.

4. Any credit for reducing costs will go to the budget manager and the accounting department.

These are logical reasons. Add to these the fact that most people hate change and the inevitable rumors that accompany a major system change (for example, 50 per cent of the supervisors are going to be replaced). It is no surprise that the introduction of a budgetary control system is usually looked upon as a little less than desirable by line management.

Although the subject of interpersonal relationships between line supervisors and budget personnel is generally outside of the scope of this book, no treatment of budgetary control is complete without at least recognizing the effect that these relationships have on the budget system. Some general rules for budget people to consider in their relations with line personnel are:

1. Line personnel should be informed of the plans, objectives, and timing of the system. Line supervision should be brought into the picture as soon as possible and as much as possible.

2. Budget personnel should lean over backward to be scrupulously honest in all their relationships with line personnel. Since the line personnel are probably suspicious of the motives of the budget people to begin with, any overt act that could be construed as dishonest can have serious repercussions on the installation of the system.

3. It must be recognized that the line personnel believe that the installation of budgets will not benefit them. Frequently, this belief is held with amazing tenacity. It will probably never be possible to convince all line personnel of the desirability of the control system until after it is installed. (Some, perhaps, not even then.) Most descriptions of good budgetary control techniques call for coordinating the program with all personnel affected by the system. This is good advice and one of the principal axioms of budgetary control. The real problem, however, is *when to stop coordinating.* When a system is first being installed, many line supervisors believe that it is to their personal advantage to resist the installation. With this conflict of interests, it may be impossible to get any kind of agreement from them. At some point it is necessary to stop coordinating and get the system in operation. It is usually desirable to establish a fairly tight timetable and coordinate the budget plans to the extent *practical within this timetable.*

4. After an effective budgetary control system has been operating for some period of time, all good line personnel will see its advantages. Like a report card, it is a means for indicating superior performance. This aspect must be carefully guarded. The budgets and reports should indicate the operating performance objectively and fairly.

BUDGET PREPARATION

Another axiom of effective budgeting technique is that the initial budget should be prepared by the person responsible for operating under it. This means that the budget must be built from the bottom up and the department manager or foreman of each department is responsible for setting the basic departmental budget. The accounting department and, frequently, the industrial engineering department provide assistance. Particularly when a budget system is first installed, a great deal of help may be required. (Although the accounting and industrial engineering departments are supposed to provide only assistance, in actual fact, they usually exercise considerable influence on the efficiency level.) The final budget should, however, be acceptable to the person responsible for meeting it.

The plant manager reviews the departmental budgets, makes whatever adjustments he believes are appropriate (after talking to the people involved), and sends the plant budget on to corporate management (or divisional management if the plant is part of a division of a larger company). At this level, the budget is again reviewed, perhaps adjusted and approved. The budget preparation and approval procedure is somewhat like a pyramid. The department budgets are approved by the plant manager. Next comes the plant budgets which are approved by the division manager. All of the division budgets are combined and submitted to the corporate president. Finally all of the approved divisional budgets are combined into a single corporate budget.

In summary, the budget preparation procedure is as follows:

1. The initial budget is prepared at the lowest level of responsibility.

2. The budget is reviewed and approved at each level of responsibility. At each level it may be adjusted but, hopefully, only with the permission of the individual whose budget is being changed.

3. Although the accounting department does much of the actual budget preparation, it is always done by working with the people involved. A budget imposed on a department by the accounting staff, for example, is almost universally condemned.

BUDGET REVIEW

Because the operating budget is used to evaluate the line manager, it must represent a reasonable "task." A budget that can be met by an inefficient manager is hardly a satisfactory basis for evaluating the effectiveness of cost performance. Furthermore, performance is frequently measured on a relative basis; that is, even though the budget is supposed to be a more or less absolute goal, there is always a tendency to evaluate the budget performance of a department manager in relation to what others in the group have done. If a budget performance report is to be an effective evaluation tool, the budget must not only represent a reasonable task but the degree of task should be as comparable for all departments. Frequently one of the most difficult problems in administering an overhead budget system is establishing a reasonable and equal task among the departments.

In general, the determination of an "adequate task" is a serious problem only in manufacturing overhead budgets. Direct material and direct labor are subject to objective measures, but exact techniques for measuring the efficiency of overhead costs are generally not readily available. Unfortunately, however, overhead costs are frequently the most important segment of controllable manufacturing cost, often four or more times as large as direct labor. The problems associated with establishing an "adequate task" for manufacturing overhead budgets are considered in this section.

The principal reason for the difficulty in establishing an "adequate task" is that a conflict of interests exists between the plant manager and his supervisors (or the divisional manager and the plant manager), when line management is evaluated on cost performance rather than profit performance. If a plant is a profit center, the plant manager is responsible for profit performance. It is to his interest to have as effective an overhead budget as possible. Top management is not concerned with the overhead budget, so long as the profits are adequate. If, however, the plant is not a profit center, the evaluation of the plant manager will be based on his cost performance. In most cases, this will be performance against his operating budget. Under this condition, it is to the benefit of the plant manager to have as loose a budget as possible. Precisely the same condition applies to the department manager; the easier the budget, the better will be the performance.

This conflict of interest does not mean that a profit center system should be universally adopted. Although the criteria for the adoption of a decentralized profit control system are outside of the scope of this book, it can be stated that there are many important considerations in decentralized profit control systems of which this conflict of interest is only one. Also, it is almost impossible to avoid this conflict at some level. Even if the plant is made into a profit center, it may be impractical to make most of the departments within the plant into profit centers. *The important point in budget administration is to recognize the points where these conflicts of interest exist and to take appropriate safeguards.*

The appropriate safeguard is the budget review. Although the budget must be prepared by the plant manager and approved by top management, between the preparation and approval there must be some independent group who analyze the budget and otherwise provide staff assistance to top management in evaluating the adequacy of the proposed budget. This function usually comes under the controller except where there is a separate budget department not reporting to the controller.

The following techniques are used by budget departments (frequently with the help of the industrial engineering department) to insure an adequate and equal task for each budget.

1. *Engineering standards.* For indirect labor, this requires a study of the specific people needed at each volume, using industrial engineering "manning" charts. Through these charts, the precise number of people required for each function is established. For other costs, the actual level should be determined, to the extent practical, by industrial engineering studies.

This method is, of course, the best one for establishing an adequate level of budget efficiency. Unfortunately it has three drawbacks that limit its use in actual business situations:

a. It is expensive and time-consuming;

b. Frequently it cannot be done by the budget personnel who have the primary responsibility for analyzing the budget proposal;

c. Industrial engineering techniques have not been developed to measure many overhead expenses. Consequently, the valuation of these costs must still depend heavily on some other method.

2. *Comparison among departments or plants.* It is sometimes possible to compare directly specific kinds of overhead costs among departments or plants. This usually requires using a common denominator such as direct labor hours. For example, Plant A may have budgeted maintenance expense of $1.00 per direct labor hour; Plant B, $1.10; Plant C, $1.20; and Plant D, $2.00. This comparison does not mean that Plant D's budget is inefficient; it does mean, however, that the level of expense should be justified by unique circumstances. Comparisons of this kind are used to isolate the questionable areas of the budget. The budget analyst, then, goes back to the plant and either obtains a good reason for the difference or tries to get the plant personnel to change the budget. If he can accomplish neither, he reports to his supervisor that the budget is not acceptable.

This method is perhaps one of the most commonly used means for evaluating a budget. It has three limitations, however, as follows:

a. It can only be used where there is a number of roughly comparable budget units;

b. In almost all cases, each budget unit will have unique conditions that make comparison in some area of expense meaningless;

c. It will not expose a situation where one plant, because of a unique condition, should have a significantly lower cost than others.

3. *Comparison with past performance.* The most commonly used method for evaluating a budget is to compare the proposed budget with the expense level actually experienced during the previous period (usually a year). In making this comparison, it is necessary to adjust the previous year's costs to reflect the current year's conditions. For example, adjustments are made for increases in direct labor rates or prices of indirect materials and supplies; the previous year's actual costs are adjusted to standard volume; sometimes adjustments are also made for unusual changes in operating conditions that have occurred since the previous year (for example, changes in the products manufactured).

The important point about these adjustments is that they should be clearly explained and usually developed on a separate schedule. Where the budget evaluation is based on the previous year's actual costs, this schedule is perhaps the most important one in the entire budget proposal. Incorrect adjustments can result in a budget proposal appearing satisfactory when, in fact, it is not. For example, an overstatement of the adjustment for increases in wage rates will increase the previous year's adjusted expense. If the budget proposal is equal to this adjusted amount, it appears that the budget proposal is at last year's efficiency. In fact, the new budget is at a lower efficiency. If the adjustment for wages had been correct, this would have been evident.

The principal weaknesses of this method of evaluation are:

a. It will show only whether the proposed budget represents cost levels that are more or less efficient than the previous year's actual experience. It does not indicate that the absolute level of costs are efficient. The more efficient manager will frequently end up with the most difficult budget.

b. The correctness of the adjustment to bring the previous year's expenses up to present conditions is sometimes difficult to evaluate, particularly when technical production or design changes are involved. (These adjustments cannot be eliminated because, in most cases, comparisons are meaningless without them.)

4. *Arbitrary reductions.* A method sometimes used to try to reach an efficient cost level is to make mandatory each year that the budget level be a designated per cent lower than the previous year's actual cost. The principle is that by constantly tightening the task, the line managers will be forced to use maximum ingenuity and effort in controlling costs.

This method has some obvious disadvantages and should be used with great care. For example, it tends to favor the department that was most inefficient at the time the budget system was installed. The most important drawback, however, is that it can give the line manager an incentive to hold back cost saving plans. If the expected reduction is five per cent a year, it will be to a manager's interest to hold back until the following year further cost savings as soon as he knows he can attain his present budget.

In general, this method is not satisfactory and should be used only under unusual circumstances. For example, it may be useful for the first year or two after a budget system has been installed until more objective techniques can be developed.

In actual business situations, a good budget analyst will use parts of all four of these methods in analyzing operating budgets. The important point to remember is that since all these methods have weaknesses, appropriate safeguards should be employed against them.

BUDGET APPROVAL

The usual procedure is for the budget director or controller to review the budget with the plant manager (or, within a plant, with the department foreman) and to try to settle any areas of disagreement. In the exceptional cases where agreement cannot be reached, the controller or budget director should submit a report to management, recommending that the budget not be approved and explaining why. At this point, it is up to management to decide whether or not to accept the budget. (It is evident that if the budget is accepted against the advice of the controller, his position will be considerably weakened the following year.)

Below is a summary of the people involved in the preparation and approval of the overhead budget.

	Department (a) Budget	Plant Budget	Division Budget
Person responsible for its preparation	Department superintendent or foreman	Plant manager	Divisional manager
Group responsible for assisting in the preparation	Plant accounting and industrial engineering	Plant accounting and industrial engineering	Divisional accounting and industrial engineering
Person responsible for approving budget .	Plant manager	Divisional manager	Corporate president
Group responsible for providing staff assistance for evaluating the budget	Plant controller or plant budget director	Divisional controller or divisional budget director	Corporate controller or corporate budget director

(a) Throughout this book a department is considered to be a subdivision of a plant when the term is used in connection with a manufacturing operation.

The type of review described in this section is generally undertaken only where the evaluation of operating management is made on the basis of cost performance, rather than profit performance. If the division was responsible for profit performance, the overhead budget would be part of the profit budget (described in Chapter 8) and would not be given the intensive review that is required when the divisional manager is evaluated on the basis of his cost performance.

The intensive review described in this section is not required in all companies. In small plants, evaluating a budget is usually much easier and complicated procedures are unnecessary. The same is true of larger plants whose costs are principally of a fixed nature. For example, the costs of some chemical processing plants are essentially fixed by the design of the plant, and the plant manager has little control over the day-to-day cost levels. In this case, budget review procedures will be quite simple.

LEVEL OF BUDGET EFFICIENCY

In administering a budgetary control system, it is usually desirable to define as precisely as possible the efficiency to be reflected in the budget. The levels of efficiency may be divided into two types, as follows (of course, an indefinite number of gradations in between these two levels are possible):

1. Generally attainable;
2. Attainable only when all costs are at a maximum reasonable efficiency.

The first level is the expected actual costs, excluding any obvious inefficiencies. A budget of this kind is defined as "attainable under reasonably efficient operations." It is expected that these budgets will normally be equaled or bettered.

The second level is known as a "tight" budget. That is, it reflects a degree of efficiency that, though possible to attain, can be done only with difficulty (and, to some extent, luck). It is expected that this budget will not normally be attained and, when it is, will reflect outstanding cost performance.

The choice of the level to be used will depend upon the circumstances surrounding the individual case. Some of the advantages and disadvantages of these two levels must be considered.

The principal advantage of the generally attainable level is that it is acceptable to line management. The disadvantage is that it provides for a kind of "average" efficiency. Average efficiency is hard to define and, therefore, allows considerable latitude among different budgets. It makes it difficult for the budget analyst to show where certain parts of the budget should be tightened because, if a budget is to be generally attainable, it must provide some allowance for inefficiency. The problem facing the budget analyst is "How much inefficiency?" Another related disadvantage is that a loose budget does not provide the incentive for cost control that a tighter budget does.

The advantages of defining the budget level as "attainable only when all costs are at a maximum reasonable efficiency" are: (1) the budget analyst is better able to evaluate the degree of task reflected in the proposed budget; and (2) there is a greater incentive to minimize costs. If it can be shown that the efficiency reflected in the budget proposal for a particular expense is less than reasonably possible, the budget level should be adjusted downward. There is much less room for judgment than when some degree of inefficiency must be allowed. In addition, a tight budget generally provides a greater incentive for cost reduction than a loose budget.

The principal disadvantage of the "tight" budget is that it is harder to get operating people to accept it. They tend to oppose a budget that they almost certainly will not be able to meet. Another disadvantage is that it must be adjusted if it is to be used in planning. Because the budgets at this level will not be attained consistently, the budgeted amounts must be increased to be used for forecasting profits, cash planning, or forward product decisions.

In general, the tight budget is more effective for cost control. More important, however, is not whether there is a tight or a loose budget but that everyone knows what is expected. In many companies there is considerable confusion because no definition of the level of expected efficiency is available. Some companies have, however, operated successfully without any explicit definition of budget efficiency because over the years a working arrangement has been reached between the operating and staff personnel. In systems where there is no definition, it is necessary to determine whether some implicit definition is in effect, whether it is being applied uniformly, and whether management actually understands and agrees with the level being used.

There is a cliché commonly used in budget administration that states that people can be motivated by either "a carrot or a whip." This cliché means that people can be motivated either by hope of reward or fear of punishment. In most modern budget philosophy, the reward incentive is considered superior, although it is far from universally applied in modern business. An argument frequently asserted in favor of the attainable budget is that it represents a "carrot" while the tight budget is a "whip." Nothing could be further from the truth. The "carrot" and "whip" techniques of administration have nothing to do with the degree of difficulty of the budget. These techniques apply to what management does with the budget performance reports. For example, a man could be rewarded if his off-budget performance was less than 10 per cent; this is the carrot technique. In another company, a man may be severely reprimanded if he did not better his budget. Even if the budget was not difficult to attain, this is the whip technique. These administrative techniques are quite apart from the level of efficiency reflected in the operating budgets.

FUNCTIONS OF THE CONTROLLER IN THE ADMINISTRATION OF OPERATING BUDGETS

The functions of the controller in the administration of operating budgets have been discussed in the preceding pages. The purpose of this section is to summarize these functions. The controller[1] is generally responsible for:

1. Designing, installing, and subsequently administering the budget system;
2. Providing assistance to line personnel in completing the budget forms and preparing the budget presentation;
3. Providing staff assistance to management by analyzing the budget proposals and recommending acceptance or rejection (Except in

[1] It is assumed that the budget function is under the controller, rather than under a budget director reporting to someone else.

unusual circumstances, the controller will recommend acceptance because any disagreement is normally resolved *before* the budget is presented);

4. Preparing and analyzing budget performance reports and developing explanations of variances.

Overhead Expense Budget Performance Reports

The purpose of this part of the chapter is to describe a typical manufacturing overhead expense budget performance report and to explain the general principles of expense budget reporting. The reporting of direct material or direct labor need not be considered here because, in most standard cost systems, these reports are provided as part of the variance analysis. (A more sophisticated system of material cost control, however, is described in Chapter 10.)

THE PREPARATION OF THE BUDGET PERFORMANCE

The preparation of a budget performance report can probably be best explained by an example. The approved budget for Department X in Plant Y of the ABC Company is as follows:

ABC COMPANY

Plant Y, Department X

1962 Overhead Expense Budget

at Standard Volume

Account Series		Fixed Costs	Variable Costs	Total Costs	Variable Authorization Rate (Variable Cost ÷ Standard Direct Labor)
No.	Name				
100	Indirect Labor	$60,000	$60,000	$120,000	.500
200	Supplies	1,200	6,000	7,200	.050
300	Tools	3,600	3,000	6,600	.025
400	Utilities	4,800	12,000	16,800	.100
500	Maintenance	12,000	24,000	36,000	.200
600	Fringe Benefits	12,000	36,000	48,000	.300
700	Scrap	—	24,000	24,000	.200
800	Depreciation & Property Taxes	30,000	—	30,000	—
	Total Overhead	$123,600	$165,000	$288,600	1.375
	Standard Direct Labor			$120,000	

In January of 1962, the standard direct labor cost of the products produced in Department X was $12,000. Actual costs were as follows: direct labor, $12,500; indirect labor, $12,000; supplies, $750; tools, $500;

utilities, $1,750; maintenance, $2,000; fringe benefits, $4,900; scrap, $2,500; depreciation and property taxes, $2,500.

The budgeted authorization for each expense series is calculated by adding 1/12 of the annual fixed expense to the variable overhead authorization. The latter is calculated by multiplying the variable authorization rate by the *standard* direct labor at actual volume. (Using the actual direct labor would provide the inefficient manager with additional overhead authorization.)

A typical budget performance report is similar to the following exhibit:

ABC COMPANY

Plant Y, Department X

January, 1962, Direct Labor and Overhead Performance

Account Series				Budget over/ (under) Actual	
No.	Name	Budget	Actual	Amount	%
100	Indirect Labor	$11,000	$12,000	$(1,000)	(9)%
200	Supplies	700	750	(50)	(7)
300	Tools	600	500	100	17
400	Utilities	1,600	1,750	(150)	(9)
500	Maintenance	3,400	2,000	1,400	40
600	Fringe Benefits	4,600	4,900	(300)	(7)
700	Scrap	2,400	2,500	(100)	(4)
800	Depreciation & Property Taxes	2,500	2,500	—	—
		$26,800	$26,900	$(100)	—
	Direct Labor	12,000	12,500	(500)	(4)
	Total Overhead and Labor	$38,800	$39,400	$(600)	(2)%

TIMING OF BUDGET PERFORMANCE REPORTS

The timing of budget performance reports will, of course, depend upon management's uses of these reports. A typical report schedule is as follows:

Daily—Direct labor performance by productive department.

Weekly—Estimated direct labor and overhead performance reports for all departments.

Monthly—A preliminary direct labor and overhead performance report for the month by department and for the total plant. (This would be prepared before the books are closed and would be partially forecast.) Final monthly and year-to-date performance reports for all departments. Final monthly and year-to-date performance report for the plant.

All of these reports are not always necessary. A common fallacy is that the department manager always depends upon his performance report to know what has happened and, consequently, what action must be taken. Very often, the department manager knows daily approximately what his cost performance will be because he keeps a rough estimate. The performance report only makes his rough estimate more precise. In this case, the manager does not need to get daily or even weekly reports because he does not use these reports as a basis for action. The performance report is used to evaluate his performance, after the fact, and to let his superior know when something is going wrong. (If things are going very wrong, it would be very surprising if the department manager's superiors did not already know about it.)

A method that makes it possible to publish a report shortly after the end of the month is to forecast the last few days of the month and publish a preliminary report. A final report is subsequently published, based on the actual data. In most cases, the advantage in timing far offsets the decrease in accuracy resulting from forecasting part of the cost performance.

DETAIL INCLUDED IN BUDGET PERFORMANCE REPORTS

Another question with respect to budget performance reports concerns the detail to be included. In general, it should be by expense series, by department. There can be offsetting performance factors and management needs to know something about what has caused the off-standard performance. In the ABC Company example, the large favorable variance in maintenance nearly offset all of the other unfavorable variances. This is important for management to know.

To go below expense series commonly results in too much detail. If this information is useful, however, there is no objection to breaking out the cost performance further. In many cases, it is useful to show certain major expense items separately.

The reports are normally prepared by responsibility center. Frequently, partial reports will go to the foreman covering only the expenses over which he has control. The arguments for this are: (1) the foreman should not be confused by expenses which he cannot control; and (2) the variances in the non-controllable accounts may appear to be much larger than those in the controllable accounts. This may lead the foreman to conclude that the expenses that he controls are relatively unimportant. The argument for including all expenses is that the foreman should be aware of the total amount of money being spent in his department.

There is no one answer to this problem. Either method can be satisfactory. The essential feature is to keep the reports as simple and understandable as possible. If the foreman cannot understand the report, it is generally worthless; if he can understand it, the inclusion or exclusion of non-controllable costs is not likely to change the effectiveness of the report.

1. *Include an annual forecast.* A budget performance report is almost always improved by including a forecast of what is expected to happen during the remainder of the year. This forecast indicates to management whether or not action should be taken about the off-standard conditions. If the off-standard results from a seasonal factor, for example, the annual forecast will probably show that by the end of the year the expenses will be at budget levels. This indicates to management that it need not be concerned about the monthly off-standard. The annual forecast also indicates to management *when* to be concerned. If an off-standard condition is expected to become significantly worse before the end of the year, management is forewarned.

2. *Include an explanation of variance.* All budget reports should be accompanied by a letter explaining the reasons for the variances from budget, and the corrective actions being taken, as well as answering any other questions that the report is likely to raise.

3. *Review the budget performance reports regularly.* The principal purpose of the expense budget is to motivate the line manager to maintain an efficient operation. The budget will be effective in motivating the manager only if he believes that it is being used by his superiors. The budget performance report should, therefore, be reviewed regularly with the people involved. Monthly cost meetings have proved to be a very effective device in many companies. At such meetings, the cost performance of each department is reviewed by the entire group (headed, of course, by the plant manager).

SUMMARY

The principal problems with respect to operating budgets occur in the area of manufacturing overhead costs. Consequently, the discussion of operating budgets has been mainly concerned with manufacturing overhead budgets.

There are three major problem areas in manufacturing overhead budgets:

1. The determination of the relationship between the amount of overhead expense and the volume of production;
2. The administration of the budgetary control system. Of particular difficulty is the establishment of an efficient "task" in the approved budget;
3. The establishment of an adequate reporting system.

In establishing an effective manufacturing overhead budgetary control system, sufficient time and attention must be directed to each of these areas. Conversely, the effectiveness of an established budgetary control system can be evaluated in terms of how well these three areas are being covered.

CHAPTER SEVEN

Budgetary Control (Part II)

PROGRAMMED BUDGETS

As stated in Chapter 6, a programmed expense is one that is subject to management's discretion within a reasonable range. It includes administrative expenses, research and development cost, and merchandising expense. Management must decide periodically how much should be spent in each of these areas. The purpose of a programmed budget proposal is to assist management in making these decisions. The subsequent budget performance reports are designed to make certain that the actual expenditures are consistent with the amounts approved by management.

A programmed budget is quite different from an operating budget. A common reason for an ineffective budgetary control system is treating these two kinds of budgets in the same way. The differences between them must be recognized in the budgetary control system and different procedures must be employed for each type.

Administration of Programmed Budgets

THE DECISION TO BE MADE

The decision that management must make with respect to a programmed budget is entirely different from the decision that it must make with respect to an operating budget. In the latter, management must decide whether the proposed operating budget represents a reasonable and fair task for the coming year. In the former, management must decide how much, if anything, should be done in each area of programmed expense. Therefore, when a budget proposal is presented, management should be provided with all available information useful in making the decision on the magnitude of the job to be performed.

In general, information supposedly indicating the level of efficiency is not applicable because evaluating the efficiency of a programmed budget is usually an impossible task. Only in the exceptional circumstance is management in a position to evaluate the efficiency of, for example, the research department, the legal department, or the finance staff. The nature of the activities that create programmed expenses are such that for the most part they are not subject to usual efficiency evaluation. Management must rely on the director of each of these activities to get the most for each dollar spent.

In spite of these considerations, however, a typical budget proposal for a programmed expense will include a breakdown of the number of people by classification, the expense by each account, and a history of these costs for several years, all in great detail. Frequently, there is hardly any information that will aid management in making an intelligent decision. (This is discussed under specific types of programmed budgets.) As a result, management must either rubber-stamp its approval or try to question individual expense items. The latter is usually a hopeless task. If the budget proposal has been prepared carefully, any individual expense can be justified (whether or not it is really justifiable). Furthermore, if management reduces a budget arbitrarily in one year, it can expect to receive a budget proposal the following year that contains sufficient "water" so that a reduction creates no hardship. The following questions should be asked with respect to a programmed budget proposal:

1. What are the precise decisions that management should make?
2. Does the proposal include all the available information pertinent to making these decisions?
3. Does the proposal include irrelevant information which, at best, will tend to obscure the real issues?

THE METHOD OF COST CONTROL

The method of cost control in a programmed budget is also quite different from the method used in an operating budget. The latter minimizes operating costs by setting a standard and reporting actual costs against this standard. Costs are minimized by *motivating* line managers to maintain maximum efficiency and by giving management a means of evaluating the effectiveness of line management. (The evaluation helps minimize costs by enabling management to promote the most effective and to replace the least effective.) A programmed budget, on the other hand, allows management to control costs by *participating in the planning.* Costs are controlled by deciding what projects should be undertaken. This difference in method will normally result in a difference in the level of efficiency reflected in the two types of budgets. In the case of operating budgets, the level of efficiency represented by the standards should be difficult to attain. For example, a budget that is impossible to attain is quite satisfactory if everyone understands this fact and acts accordingly. Under almost all circumstances, as explained in the preceding chapter, it is usually necessary to have some "task" in an operating budget. A programmed budget, on the other hand, should *reflect the best possible estimate of the actual cost.* Although this distinction may not appear to be important, there can be undesirable consequences if it is not kept in mind. For example, if a programmed budget is supposed to include a "task," the actual expenses may end up considerably higher than the budget. If this happens, management may have made an incorrect decision. Had the correct amounts been reflected in the budget, the decision might have been quite different. The same consideration applies to a budget that is too loose. Management may reject certain projects because they appear to be too costly when, in fact, the estimated costs have been overstated.

There is one school of thought in budgeting philosophy that believes categorically that a tight budget is a good budget. The theory behind this philosophy is that a tight budget will be instrumental in putting on more pressure to reduce costs than one that is more easily attainable. (In general, the author subscribes to this theory when it pertains to operating budgets. Although even here one can always find exceptions.) When this philosophy is carried over to programmed budgets, however, it is certainly not correct. It is easy to reduce costs in a programmed budget by reducing the magnitude of the job to be done. In this case, the individual responsible for spending the money, instead of management, is making the decision as to the job to be done. This is all right *only if* management explicitly delegates this decision.

The general rule then is that programmed budgets should reflect as closely as possible *the actual costs of doing the job.* A deviation from this rule should be backed by adequate reasons and this condition should be known to management when the budget is presented for approval.

REPORTS

In programmed budgets, the performance report is used to insure that the budget commitment will not be exceeded without management's knowledge. It is not a means of evaluating the effectiveness of the manager in cost control. (This is in complete contrast to the operating budget which *is* designed to be a tool to help management evaluate the effectiveness of line management in cost control.)

Because the two types of budgets are confused, management will sometimes treat a programmed budget report as an indication of efficiency. If this is done, the people responsible for the programmed budget will be motivated to spend less than budgeted. This can be accomplished either by proposing a budget that can be bettered or by subsequently reducing the size of the job to be done. This is, of course, undesirable for the reasons given in the preceding section. This pressure toward lower costs may possibly result in the same job done for less money, either by increasing productivity or eliminating unnecessary operations, but management cannot depend on this. In an operating budget, this is the logical way to better the budget. In a programmed budget, it is the most difficult way. In any event, since management can so rarely gauge the efficiency of a programmed budget, there is little point in trying to increase this efficiency by such indirect methods as rewarding executives who spend less than budget.

Control over the actual expenditures can be exercised by requiring that management approval be obtained before the budget can be overrun. Customarily a certain percentage (say, five per cent) is allowed without additional approval. If the budget includes the best estimate of actual costs, there is an even chance that it will be overrun somewhat. If approval is required before any overrun, the budget proposals will come in on the high side.

In summary, then, the budget reports for a programmed budget should be used to follow up on the original estimates. Control is exercised by requiring additional approval if the original budget is to be overrun by more than a given per cent.

FIXED AND FLEXIBLE BUDGETS

Programmed budgets are almost always of the fixed kind, whereas operating budgets are usually of the flexible kind. For this reason, there is a tendency to divide budgets into fixed and flexible and to consider the former as programmed and the latter as operating. Although these categories may be correct most of the time, they are not always right; certain operating budgets can be fixed. Because operating budgets are treated differently from programmed budgets, all fixed budgets must not be treated as programmed budgets. In deciding what budget procedure to follow, first decide whether an expense falls into the operating category or the programmed category. Next, decide whether a fixed budget or a flexible budget will provide the best control. If a flexible budget is best, apply the criteria listed in Chapter 6 to see if it is practicable.

Programmed expenses will almost always be fixed. About the only exception is the undertaking of a project depending on some condition uncertain at the time of budget approval (such as being able to hire a particular kind of scientist). In this case, the project may be tentatively authorized. Even here, it is not a flexible budget in the sense used in this book; it is only a fixed budget with a tentative additional authorization.

The conclusion is that operating budgets should be flexible if establishing them on this basis is practicable. If not, they should be fixed, but the element of efficiency should still be present because the job to be done is already defined. Programmed budgets will almost always be fixed in nature. Budgets should not be divided into fixed budgets and flexible budgets, however, for the purpose of presentation and approval; the meaningful distinction is between operating budgets and programmed budgets.

Types of Programmed Budgets

In general, programmed budgets will cover all expenses reflected on the typical income statement between the gross profit and profit before taxes. These are administrative expenses, merchandising expenses, and research and development costs. Although this classification is arbitrary, it is sufficiently accurate to be used in nearly every situation. There can, of course, be some element of programmed expense in the operating budgets. For example, a plant manager may undertake a project to develop a new production process. On the other hand, there are operational aspects of most programmed expenses. (These will be discussed under the specific kinds of programmed budgets.) Nevertheless, the amount of programmed expense in the operating category is usually quite small, and vice versa. Where the amount is small, little is gained by isolating the operating-type expenses that are part of the programmed expenses. Where they are significant, however, they should be treated separately.

ADMINISTRATIVE BUDGETS

The administrative budget includes the costs of staff operations, excluding sales and research. Normally administrative expenses include the cost of the offices of the top-line executives (president and executive vice-president), finance, industrial relations, manufacturing staff (to the extent this is separated from the plant activities), legal department, and so forth. The budget procedure for controlling administrative expense will vary from an informal discussion between the president and the staff executive involved to an elaborate, formal presentation of proposed expenditures for the coming year. In a small company, the president uses most of his staff daily and can determine from personal observation what they are doing and whether it is worth the expense. The only use for a budget in this case is to formalize the decision-making and planning.

In medium- or large-sized businesses, however, the operating executive knows about activities being undertaken by the staff offices only in a general way. Moreover, he frequently has only a remote idea of the precise purpose of many of these activities and the related costs. A good budget proposal will provide top management with information on the projects that are to be undertaken as well as the cost of these projects. This information should be presented in such a way that management can make intelligent decisions. This means that where no decisions are required, management needs only summary information. Where decisions are required, management should be given all information relevant to the decision. For example, the cost of the accounting functions required for the certification of the financial statements, the reports to the Securities and Exchange Commission, and the reports to the tax authorities can be treated in total in preparing a finance staff budget because management has no real decision to make. (These activities are a necessary part of being in business.) The addition of a computer analysis department, however, should include a fairly detailed description of purposes and costs. (The marginal costs of this department will be used in the presentation because these are the relevant costs to management.)

For each staff department, a complete administrative budget proposal consists of the following:

1. A section covering the basic costs of the department. This includes all of the costs of being "in business" plus the costs of all activities which *must* be undertaken and for which no general management decisions are required.
2. A section covering all other activities of the department. This includes a description of the purposes and the marginal costs of each activity. The quantity of detail depends upon the ability of management to make a decision about the activity and the amount of money involved. For example, a limited amount of detail may be enough for a financial analysis department because management does not need to review its functions each year. Proposed additions to its activities may be all that is needed.
3. A section explaining the activities that would be curtailed or cancelled if the budget were reduced 5 per cent, 10 per cent, or 15 per cent.
4. A section explaining the activities that would be increased or started if the budget could be increased 5 per cent or 10 per cent.

Clearly, all four of these sections will be required only where the departmental budget is large and where management wishes to decide on the extent of the activities of the department. For other departments, the amount of detail is dependent upon the importance of the expenditures and the desires of management. The important point, however, is that *if* management is expected to decide the level of administrative activity, the presentation should be aimed at providing the information needed for an intelligent decision.

Once an administration budget has been approved, a monthly report of actual expenditures against budget is usually prepared. This report is not designed to measure efficiency but to keep management informed about any possible under- or overruns. There are few accounting problems associated with administrative budget reports. The actual costs are always kept in at least the same detail as that required by the budget. The budget reports are designed for the most part to help the staff executive control his costs. Top management usually needs only totals by department.

In some cases management may wish to check actual costs by activity. In this case, some changes in the accounting system may be required to obtain this information. Much of the confusion in budget proposals arises because many accounting systems are designed to maintain administrative expenses by cost categories (for example, supervisory expense, clerical expense, office supplies, depreciation) instead of by type of activity. Information on cost by specific activities is sometimes not available. In most instances, however, it can be readily approximated from the accounting records. Because the real control of administrative expense occurs at the time of budget approval, the accounting system must be designed so that the information required for an intelligent decision is available, either directly from the books or through a special study.

Sometimes administrative costs contain elements of operating budgets. For example, an accounting department normally handles accounts receivable and an industrial relations department handles the processing of new employees. It is desirable to separate these expenses under two conditions: (1) when the amount of costs varies with the volume of operations; and (2) when the amount of variance is significant in relation to the total budget. When these two conditions are met, a flexible budget arrangement to authorize these expenses prevents an off-budget performance over which the staff executive has no control.

In summary, the control of administration expense occurs at the point when the budget is approved. Most of the effort, therefore, should be made at this time to insure the best decisions. Performance reports are useful and necessary to help the staff executive keep within his budget and to assure top management that the budget commitments are met.

Performance reports are *not* useful in evaluating the efficiency of the staff executive.

RESEARCH AND DEVELOPMENT COSTS

The principles governing the preparation of budget proposals and the subsequent reporting of actual costs against budget are the same for research and development budgets as for administrative budgets. Because of the differences in the nature of these costs, however, somewhat different problems occur. These differences are:

1. Research and development activities are more technical than administrative activities and management is frequently in a poorer position to make decisions in this area.

2. Research directors tend to be (but by no means always are) less acquainted with the general management problems than administrative staff executives. Also, they tend to be less commercially oriented.

3. An error in judgment concerning research and development activities may take longer to correct. Generally, staff activities can be increased quickly depending upon the urgency. In research activities, however, it may take several years to overcome a deficiency.

4. Large annual swings in research and development costs are generally undesirable. Because much of the expense of research departments is accounted for by the salaries of scientists and engineers (who are generally hard to find), increases or decreases in staff must be carefully planned. A company cannot expect to lay off large numbers of technical people one year when business is bad and hire an equal number of competent ones the next year when business is good.

These four differences boil down to this: In many industries, correct decisions about research and development expenditures are more vital than decisions about administrative expenditures, yet more difficult to make. Clearly, the solution to this problem (if there be a solution) is outside of the scope of budgetary control. The controller or budget director must understand the problem, however, if he is to design the most effective budgetary control system.

The minimum decision that management must make is the total amount of money to be spent on research and development. In some instances, management's only function in this area is to make this one decision. The spending of the money is left up to the director of research and development. At the other extreme, top management may approve specifically each research project to be undertaken.

The objective is to have the decision made by the person or persons best qualified. This will be different in different companies. In one company, a research director, well versed in management problems, may be the best person to make all decisions concerning the direction of research expenditures. In another company, the research director may be somewhat like the stereotype of the impractical scientist in his ivory tower; in this instance, considerable control by top management over the direction of research expenditures may be required.

In addition to the general principles applicable to programmed budgets and the specific recommendations applicable to administrative budgets, the following additional considerations apply to research and development budgets:

1. The decision as to who will decide the projects to be undertaken is of vital importance and should receive considerable attention. Each decision should be made by the best-qualified individual. This will usually mean that several people will be making decisions with respect to the research budget. The simplest division of authority is to have top management determine the total amount to be spent and the research director decide on the specific projects to be undertaken. Sometimes a committee is the most effective means for reviewing and approving proposed research projects. Such a committee will normally include the director of research, the director of sales, the director of production, and the president or executive vice-president. In businesses where research is a vital area, the research committee meets frequently (sometimes as often as every week) to consider plans.

2. In a decentralized company, there can be considerable danger of duplicate activities. Where this possibility exists, it is necessary to have a system of coordination and cooperation among the various research activities.

3. Management should decide explicitly at least how much to spend each year. In general, making this amount depend on arbitrary formulae is not advisable. For example, a company budgets research expenses equal to 2 per cent of expected sales. Although 2 per cent of sales may be the optimum expenditure for the long run, it is unlikely to be optimum each year. (In years when volume is low, it may be desirable to increase expenditures for research.) Furthermore, situations change rapidly and the optimum in one period can be quite wrong in another. In most companies, research and development is so important that at least an annual review appears to be absolutely necessary.

MERCHANDISING BUDGETS

Selling, advertising and sales promotion, and warehousing have been grouped together for consideration under the merchandising budget. Admittedly, these activities will appear in different places in different companies. Warehousing, for example, can be grouped under manufacturing.

The merchandising budget is peculiar because it includes both operating and programmed characteristics, as well as some features essentially unique to both. For convenience of treatment, the merchandising budget has been divided into three types of costs: (1) those incurred after the point of sale; (2) administrative-type expenses; and (3) advertising and sales promotion.

Expenses incurred after the sale has been made. One of the unique features of the merchandising budget is that *operating-type budgets will apply to costs incurred after the sale has been made.* For example, shipping and delivery expense, salesmen's commissions, and collection costs all occur after the sale has been made. The failure to realize this has caused much confusion in sales budgets. A manager or controller realizes that fixed budgets result in unequitable situations because, for example, a sales manager will overrun his budget for sales commissions when he has achieved higher than budgeted sales volume. The next step is frequently to try to put the entire sales budget on a variable basis. A reasonably good correlation may often be found between volume of sales and the level of sales promotion and advertising (and even the cost of sales staff). This is taken to mean that they are variable with sales. Consequently, a flexible budget is established, using manufacturing overhead budget techniques.

Flexible budgets are wrong for selling expenses that are incurred *prior* to the sale. Advertising or sales promotion expense, for example, should not be authorized on the basis of a flexible budget. A correlation between sales volume and advertising costs is caused either by the mutual growth of both expenses as a result of the growth of the company or because advertising costs have *caused* the increase in sales. It does not make sense to turn this around and say that sales volume *causes* advertising expenditures.

An operating-type budget, however, is useful in controlling expenses that are incurred *after* the sale has been made. In this case, the job to be done is determined by the volume of sales. To the extent that the volume of activity affects these costs significantly, a flexible budget authorization should be incorporated into the system. Even if establishing a flexible budget authorization is unnecessary, this part of the merchandising budget should be treated as an operating budget in that approval is based on having an efficient "task," and the budget performance reports for this segment of the merchandising budget will reflect operating efficiency.

Frequently, the total amount of operating-type expenses included in the merchandise budget is not large enough to warrant separate treatment. In this case, sales commissions can be put on a flexible basis by having the budget authorization equal the actual expense. All other costs incurred after the point of sale can be treated in the same way as the other programmed costs.

Administrative-type costs. Most merchandising budgets include administrative-type costs. There is usually a basic staff plus other peripheral activities (for example, advertising research). The former is necessary to stay in business but the latter can be changed by management decree. This part of the sales budget should be handled exactly like any other administrative staff budget.

Advertising and sales promotion. Most merchandising budgets include proposed expenditures for advertising and sales promotion. In some respects, the problem of approving these costs is similar to the problem of approving research expenditures in that they are technical in nature and, to some extent, management has to accept on faith that they are necessary. The problems of advertising and sales promotion, however, are sufficiently unique that some general rules can be laid down:

1. The usual objective is to advertise as long as a dollar of advertising expense returns more than a dollar in marginal contribution. This means that the important decision is *when to stop advertising.* For management to be able to make, or even help make, such a decision it should be provided with any information that will illuminate this problem. Management should also be informed if there is no objective information to help make this decision so that it can specifically delegate the decision to the person who has the best intuitive "feel" of the market.

2. Detailed expense information should not be provided unless it can assist management in making the necessary decisions. Too often the lack of pertinent data relevant to the effectiveness of the advertising dollar is made up for by an abundance of detail explaining where and how each dollar of advertising is to be spent. This information is frequently useless or worse than useless because it directs management's attention to the wrong problem.

3. As in research, arbitrary formulae such as percentage of sales should be avoided because it would be used to replace a necessary decision.

4. Considerable flexibility should be built into an advertising budget. For instance, the budget may be firm for the first quarter and tentative for the last three. Before each quarter, the tentative budget should be adjusted to reflect current conditions.

Summary. A merchandising budget should be considered in three parts: costs incurred after the point of sale; basic departmental and administrative costs and related staff activities; and advertising and sales promotion expense. In a small budget this detail in presenting the budget for approval and in the subsequent reporting procedure would not be warranted. In a more comprehensive budget, however, this breakdown helps to avoid a considerable amount of confusion.

Functions of the Controller in Programmed Budgets

The functions of the controller or budget director in administering programmed budgets are also quite different from those in an operating budget. In a programmed budget, the controller or budget director would generally have the following responsibilities:

1. Establishing and maintaining the mechanical features of the budgetary system (for example, setting timetables and designing forms).
2. Developing an accounting system that will provide the information that is needed for:
   (a) Preparing the budget presentation;
   (b) Controlling the actual expenditures.
3. Developing, with management, instructions for the meaningful presentation of budget proposals.
4. Assisting in the development of the budget proposal by providing the necessary accounting data and checking the proposal for accuracy and completeness.
5. Providing the staff head with accounting data to help him control his costs.
6. Preparing budget performance reports.
7. Administering the appropriate action to be taken in the event of overruns.

SUMMARY

Most of this chapter has been concerned with management's problems in connection with programmed budgets because the accounting techniques are fairly simple, but the problems to be solved by management are not. The controller's function is one of providing accounting data and keeping score. Much of the information required for making a decision is outside of the scope of the accounting data. For example, accounting data show how much advertising has cost in the past; it does not give any information on the sales that are expected to result from an increase in advertising expenditures. While these problems are principally management's, the controller must be aware of them if he is to assist by developing a meaningful budgetary control system.

In the administration of the budget, the controller has no responsibility for setting an "equal task" or an "efficient level of costs" because, except in an unusual circumstance, it is not practical to try to determine the degree of productivity or efficiency of staff operations. Management must have faith that the staff executive is doing his job as efficiently as possible. It is not normally part of the controller's job to decide how each of the other staff officers should conduct his business. If management assigns the controller to act as the staff "efficiency expert," only *then* does it become his job to recommend acceptance or rejection of budgets.

CHAPTER EIGHT

Budgetary Control (Part III)

THE PROFIT BUDGET

A profit budget is an annual management profit commitment. In addition to the profit (obtained by subtracting the budgeted costs from the budgeted revenue), the amount of investment is usually forecast and a budgeted rate of return is developed. The profit budget performs the following major functions in a control system:

1. It is used by management as a final gauge in evaluating the adequacy of the expense budgets. For example, management may have reviewed and tentatively approved all of the expense budgets. After the profit budget is prepared, however, it may become evident that the expense budgets are too high because the projected profits are too low. A further review and revision of the expense budgets will then be made to bring them into line with projected revenues.

2. Where profit responsibility is decentralized, the profit budget is the operating budget for the profit center. It is used to motivate line management to earn a satisfactory profit and subsequently to evaluate their performance. The budget is analyzed and approved in the same way as an operating expense budget. For instance, a company organized on a divisional basis with profit responsibility delegated down to the plant level will have plant profit budgets approved by divisional management

and divisional profit budgets approved by corporate management. The corporate controller will develop a corporate profit budget to be used by corporate management as a final indication of the adequacy of the divisional profit budgets. (The profit budget, like the operating budget, should represent a "task.")

3. The profit budget is used for planning and coordinating the company's activities. For example, cash forecasts are frequently made on the basis of the profit budget.

Administration of the Profit Budget

The procedure for analyzing and reviewing a profit budget is quite similar to that described for manufacturing overhead budgets. There are, however, three unique features in the profit budget to be considered: sales volume, the profit budget proposal, and the pressures for short-run profits.

1. SALES VOLUME

Corporate management may find itself in a dilemma over approving the budgeted volume of divisional sales. If the division's budgeted sales volume is conservative, the division will almost surely better the budgeted profit because sales volume usually has a greater impact on profits than any other factor. In addition, a conservative sales budget may not provide adequate incentive to the sales department. On the other hand, if the sales are budgeted optimistically high, the profits will tend to look satisfactory, even though the budgeted cost levels are excessive. Worse yet, plans based on an optimistic forecast can lead to expensive mistakes. For example, new facilities could be constructed to meet the predicted high volume of sales. Even though the company does not go this far, money may be committed and spent for programmed budgets that would be questioned if the sales volume was realistic. Furthermore, although the budgeted efficiency level of operating expenses may appear satisfactory because budgeted profits are satisfactory, at a realistic sales volume it would be evident that this is not the case. I know of several cases of divisions losing money consistently because each year profits were budgeted at a volume not attained. In one instance, not until the divisional manager reduced his standard volume to a realistic level did it become evident that this level of activity could not support the organization established for the higher anticipated volumes. When the division reorganized on a basis consistent with the realistic standard volume, it earned a profit for the first time in several years.

The divisional manager should be allowed to set his own sales volume, but *he should be expected to meet it*. The divisional manager will want to budget realistically because he will be expected to attain the budgeted volume. On the other hand, he will want to budget as high as he feels is reasonable because, if his budgeted volume is low, he might be required to take some drastic action to make his profits satisfactory. This would clearly be undesirable if he really did not expect the low volume to result. (If necessary, the problem of sales department incentive can be handled by having a separate sales target for the sales department.)

The general rule, then, should be to budget sales *as realistically as possible and to err, if at all, on the conservative side.* This can best be accomplished by making the attainment of the sales volume an important consideration in evaluating the performance of the divisional manager. In a centralized company the same rule also holds except, of course, there are no divisional managers to evaluate. The profit budget, in this case, is used to help corporate management evaluate the proposed expense budgets and to plan for the coming year. A realistic budget, on the conservative side, is also best for this purpose.

There may be exceptions to this general rule. For example, in the case of a rapidly expanding business, it may be necessary to plan on a significant annual expansion to benefit fully from expanding markets. Here it may be advantageous to "think big" when profit plans are prepared for the coming year. In general, though, this approach is dangerous. I have seen several occasions where serious management errors were covered up (at least temporarily) by constantly predicting expanding volumes that never quite materialized. (The presentation always showed that last year was bad but that next year would be the best ever.)

2. THE PROFIT BUDGET PROPOSAL

The second unique feature of profit budget administration is in the analysis and evaluation of the profit budget proposal. In a profit budget proposal, the comparison with the previous year's actual experience is usually the most important feature. (Also of importance may be the comparison of the proposed budget with the long-run plan of the division or, sometimes, the long-run profit objective.) Management knows how much was earned last year. Management also has a more or less absolute criterion for deciding on the adequacy of this profit. This criterion is the percentage return on the investment in the division. If the profit was unsatisfactory, management knows from the profit budget performance report (to be discussed later) what caused this unsatisfactory condition. At this point, management is in a good position to evaluate the profit budget proposal if the proposal is presented in terms of changes from the previous year. The profit budget proposal should show management precisely what will happen to the divisional profits next year from divisional action and what will happen to profits as a result of changes outside of the division's control.

The organization of the profit budget proposal varies greatly among companies and no attempt will be made to describe all of the possible combinations. All proposals, however, should have the following characteristics:

    a. They should start with the actual profit performance for the previous year. (Because the budget proposals are prepared in the latter part of the year, it may be necessary to use ten months' actual and two months' forecast.)

    b. All changes from last year's actual profit performance should be described in terms that management can understand. As with expense budgets, accounting details are frequently useless because they are not meaningful to management.

    c. The changes in profit performance that are to result from action of divisional management should be segregated in such a way that corporate management will be able to see what action the divisional manager is proposing to take and what effect this action will have on profits. Changes in profits resulting from changes that can be only partially controlled by divisional management should be separated. For example, a change in wage rates as a result of a corporate union agreement should be separated from an improvement in the efficiency of direct labor costs from better methods and equipment; or, changes in sales volume as a result of changes in the economy should be separated from those changes resulting from an increase in advertising.

As stated, there is a great variance in practice in profit budget proposals. Some variances result largely from differences in the capacity to control the items included in the profit budget. For example, in one company prices may be completely determined by competition and in another price levels may be partially controllable. The Westinghouse system is a good example of one company's approach to this problem. Appendix A is a description of this system by Marshall K. Evans, reprinted from the *Harvard Business Review*.

Some General Principles for Profit Budget Proposals. No attempt to cover any specific system for profit budget proposals will be made here, but some of the more useful and generally applicable principles are as follows:

    a. There are two basic methods of presenting the profit budget proposal. One method shows only profits and perhaps investments; the other method shows the changes to all of the items in the income statement. The following is an example (oversimplified) of the two methods. If three changes (increases in sales volume, price levels and wage rates, and the efficiency of labor and overhead) take place between the 1961 actual profits and the 1962 budget, method 1 would show a presentation as follows:

FIGURE 8-1:

	After Tax Profits	Investment	Rate of Return
	(000 omitted)	(000 omitted)	
1961 Actual	$1,500	$6,000	25%
Projected Increases/(Decreases):			
Increased Sales Volume	500		
Increased Costs from Changes in Price Levels and Wage Rates	(300)		
Increased Efficiency in Direct Labor and Overhead	200	500	
Net Change	400	500	
1962 Profit Budget	$1,900	$6,500	29%

Method 2 would be as follows:

FIGURE 8-2:

	1961 Actual	Increase/(Decrease) in Profits				1962 Profit Budget
		Sales Volume	Price Levels & Wage Rates	Mfg. Cost Efficiency	Total Changes	
		(000 omitted)				
Sales	$15,000	$2,800			$2,800	$17,800
Material	5,500	(1,000)	(300)		(1,300)	6,800
Direct Labor	1,700	(320)	(100)	$200	(220)	1,920
Variable Overhead ..	2,600	(480)	(100)	200	(380)	2,980
Contribution	$5,200	$1,000	$(500)	$400	$900	$6,100
Fixed Overhead	1,000					1,000
Selling Expense	500		(25)		(25)	525
Research and Development	400		(50)		(50)	450
Administrative Expense	300		(25)		(25)	325
Net Profit before Taxes	$3,000	$1,000	$(600)	$400	$800	$3,800
Income Tax	1,500	500	(300)	200	400	1,900
Profit after Tax	$1,500	$500	$(300)	$200	$400	$1,900
Investment						
Working Capital	$3,000	—	—	—	—	$3,000
Fixed Assets	3,000	—	—	500	500	3,500
TOTAL	$6,000	—	—	$500	$500	$6,500
Rate of Return	25%					

In actual business situations, the schedule on Figure 8-2 would be much wider because a considerably greater number of adjustments to the past year's profits would have to be covered.

Advocates of method 1 state that it is easier for management to understand the simpler presentation and, in any event, management is interested only in the amount of profits rather than the accounts that are affected. Advocates of method 2 state that this method gives management more information upon which to base a decision. A second advantage is that management not only approves a budgeted profit, but a specific profit budget.

The use of either method 1 or method 2 should be decided by what management wants to see. Where method 1 is used, however, the detail included in the method 2 presentation should be provided to the corporate controller's office before presentation and should be available as back-up during the budget review.

b. A preliminary profit budget should be developed segregating the changes that management can control before including profit changes from events that are difficult to predict and are, therefore, largely non-controllable by divisional management.

Westinghouse provides a good example of this segregation.[1] In the Westinghouse system the adjustments for changes in the physical volume of sales and selling prices are the last two adjustments to be made. The profit budget before these adjustments shows what the budgeted profit would have been without changes in volume and prices. Adverse changes in operating conditions are not offset, therefore, by projected improvements in sales volumes or prices. This kind of change is more difficult to forecast than other changes, yet it can have such a significant effect on profits that other more predictable management actions are obscured.

The adjustments that should be segregated depend to a great extent on the industry and the particular business. In some companies product volume and mix may be largely unpredictable, while selling prices are forecast with reasonable accuracy. In this case, the sales volume and mix are segregated (and the preliminary profit budget calculated without them) but price changes are included as part of the preliminary budgeted profits.

c. It is sometimes desirable to group and subtotal related items. For example, changes in the general level of salaries and wages, in the general level of material prices, and in the level of selling prices may be grouped together, if the policy of a company is to try to recoup in selling prices the increased costs from rising economic levels.

[1] See Appendix A.

d. The profit effect of any change will be influenced by the order in which it is considered. For example, a change in the level of variable cost will affect the contribution from additional sales and, at the same time, the additional sales will influence the amount of variable cost savings. (The savings in variable cost will be greater if calculated after the change in volume than if calculated before this change.) The usual procedure is to list the changes in reverse order of their facility in being controlled. This means that normally the changes resulting from management actions will come just before the preliminary profit budget column; the difficult-to-predict items come next; the last column is the final profit budget.

e. In most cases it will be necessary to combine items, at least for the presentation to management; otherwise, the budget presentation will become unnecessarily complicated. In combining items, care should be taken not to mislead management by offsetting important factors. For example, a general reduction in the material costs of scientific equipment should not be included in the same column as an increase in the number of people employed in the research department. The former is a change in economic levels; the latter is the result of management action.

3. PRESSURES FOR SHORT-RUN PROFITS

The third unique feature of the profit budget is the danger of undue pressure for short-term profits.

In evaluating a divisional profit budget, the programmed costs are handled differently from an expense budget evaluation. In the latter, management's problem is to decide whether or not a program or project should be undertaken. In a profit-budget evaluation, the level of the programmed costs is usually left to the discretion of the divisional manager who is responsible only for earning an adequate profit on his investment. Because profit responsibility has been decentralized, corporate management will not normally make any specific decisions concerning programmed cost. First, corporate management is usually not sufficiently familiar with the operating problems of the division to make such specific decisions; second, the purpose of decentralizing profit responsibility is to relieve top management of the necessity of making this kind of decision. In order to increase short-term profits, however, the divisional manager may be tempted to reduce the level of his programmed costs unwisely. *This is one of the dangers of the profit budget system of decentralized control.* If pressures are placed on the divisional manager to earn profits in the coming year, he may find that the easiest way is to take action that will have undesirable effects in the long run (such as reducing research and development expense). If the tenure of divisional managers are usually short (either because they are moved to other jobs or fired because results are not obtained quickly enough), the temptations to look only at the short term will be nearly overwhelming.

Although a complete consideration of the subject of decentralized profit responsibility is outside of the scope of this book, two observations may be made with respect to this aspect of the profit budget:

1. Management should consider the long-term implications of the budgeted profit. This is usually aided by having the divisions submit a long-term (about five years) profit plan along with the profit budget.

2. Particular care should be taken to review the level of critical programmed costs such as research. A low profit (or even a loss) should be considered acceptable in the short run if this appears best for the long-run welfare of the division.

Profit Budget Reporting

Reports of actual performance against the profit budget have the same general characteristics as performance reports against operating budgets. That is, the format of the reports should show clearly what has happened; they should be accompanied by a variance analysis that explains the reasons for differences from budget and answers any questions that could be raised by the report. To the extent that management makes a decision on the basis of the report, the information necessary for this should be provided as part of the report.

A profit budget report covers a wider range of management problems than an expense budget report; the analysis of budgeted performance, therefore, tends to be much more complex and to require a more sophisticated consideration of general management problems. Apart from the differences resulting from the broader coverage, two technical problems in profit budget reports must be considered:

1. The profit effect from variances in sales volume and mix should be segregated from other variances because:
    a. The effects of revenue changes are likely to be so large that they may obscure other smaller, yet more controllable, variances; and,
    b. The expense portion of the profit budget must be adjusted to the actual volume and mix to make the comparison of actual costs to budgeted costs meaningful.
2. The profit budget reporting is complicated by differences between the sales volume and the production volume.

Profit Budget Reports When Sales and Production Volumes Are Equal

The ABC Division has the following approved profit budget:

FIGURE 8-3:

ABC DIVISION

Annual Profit Budget—1962

(000 omitted)

	Part A		Part B		Part C		Total Profit Budget	
Standard Volume (units)	1,200		1,200		1,200			
	Unit	Total	Unit	Total	Unit	Total	Annual	Monthly
Sales	$1.00	$1,200	$2.00	$2,400	$3.00	$3,600	$7,200	$600
Standard Variable Cost:								
Material	.50	600	.70	840	1.50	1,800	3,240	270
Labor	.10	120	.15	180	.10	120	420	35
Variable Overhead.	.20	240	.25	300	.20	240	780	65
Total Variable Cost	$.80	$960	$1.10	$1,320	$1.80	$2,160	$4,440	$370
Contribution	$.20	$240	$.90	$1,080	$1.20	$1,440	$2,760	$230
Fixed Costs:								
Fixed Overhead ..		$300		$300		$300	$900	$75
Selling Expense [a] .		200		200		200	600	50
Administrative Expense		100		100		100	300	25
Total Fixed costs .		$600		$600		$600	$1,800	$150
Net Profit Before Taxes		$(360)		$480		$840	$960	$80

[a] For this example, selling expenses are fixed; in most business situations, there is usually a variable element to be considered.

The comparison of the actual performance with the profit budget for January can be expressed as follows:

FIGURE 8-4:

ABC DIVISION
Profit Budget Performance Report—January, 1962
(000 omitted)

	Actual	Budget	Actual Better/ (Worse) than Budget
Sales	$875	$600	$ 275
Variable Costs:			
Material	470	270	(200)
Labor	65	35	(30)
Variable Overhead	90	65	(25)
Total Variable Costs	$625	$370	$(255)
Contribution	$250	$230	$ 20
Fixed Costs:			
Fixed Overhead	75	75	—
Selling Expense	55	50	(5)
Administrative Expense	30	25	(5)
Total Fixed Costs	$160	$150	$ (10)
Net Profit	$ 90	$ 80	$ 10

This statement shows that profits are $10,000 higher than budgeted because sales are higher than budgeted, but this is about all that it shows. The only other meaningful figures on the report are the fixed cost comparisons because these are not affected by the volume of sales. The variable cost performance cannot be evaluated. A report of this kind is often meaningless; worse, it is confusing. An effective report shows the budgeted costs at actual volume and mix compared to actual costs. (The volume and mix variance will then be shown separately.) For example, the actual sales of $875,000 are assumed to be:

Part A, 100,000 units at $.90 = $90,000
Part B, 200,000 units at $2.05 = $410,000
Part C, 150,000 units at $2.50 = $375,000

         TOTAL   = $875,000

The standard variable cost at actual volume and mix for these sales is calculated as follows:

FIGURE 8-5:

Calculation of Variable Cost Variance

(000 omitted)

	Budgeted Cost at Actual Volume				Actual Cost	Favorable/ (Unfavorable) Variance
	Part A	Part B	Part C	Total		
Actual Volume (units) ..	100	200	150			
Material	$50	$140	$225	$415	$470	$(55)
Labor	10	30	15	55	65	(10)
Variable Overhead	20	50	30	100	90	10
TOTAL	$80	$220	$270	$570	$625	$(55)

The price, mix, and volume variance are calculated as follows:

(The methods used to calculate revenue variances are similar to those used in calculating the material cost variances explained in Chapter 2. Particularly note that the amount of each variance will be different if calculated in a different order.)

FIGURE 8-6:

Calculation of Price Variance

(000 omitted)

	Part A	Part B	Part C	Total
Actual Volume (units)	100	200	150	
Actual Price	$.90	$2.05	$2.50	
Budgeted Price	1.00	2.00	3.00	
Actual over/(under) Budget	(.10)	.05	(.50)	
Favorable/(Unfavorable) Price Variance	$(10)	$10	$(75)	$(75)

FIGURE 8-7:

Calculation of Mix Variance

(000 omitted)

Part	Actual Mix at Actual Volume	Budgeted Mix at Actual Volume	Actual over/ (under) Budget	Budgeted Contribution	Favorable/ (Unfavorable) Mix Variance
A	100	150	(50)	$.20	$(10)
B	200	150	50	.90	45
C	150	150	—	1.20	
TOTAL ..	450	450	—		35

FIGURE 8-8:

Volume Variance
(000 omitted)

Part	Actual Volume at Budgeted Mix	Budgeted Volume and Mix	Actual over/(under) Budget	Budgeted Contributions	Favorable/ (Unfavorable) Volume Variance
A	150	100	50	$.20	$10
B	150	100	50	.90	45
C	150	100	50	1.20	60
TOTAL	450	300	150		$115

To summarize these variances the following budgetary performance report is developed:

FIGURE 8-9:

ABC DIVISION
Profit Budget Performance Report—January, 1962
(000 omitted)

Actual Profits	$90
Budgeted Profits	80
Actual Better/(Worse) than Budget	$10

ANALYSIS OF VARIANCES
Favorable/(Unfavorable)

Revenue:

Price	$(75)	
Mix	35	
Volume	115	
Net Revenue Variance		$75

Cost:

Material	$(55)	
Labor	(10)	
Overhead	10	
Selling Expense	(5)	
Administrative Expense	(5)	
Net Cost Variance		$(65)
Net Variance		$10

Here is an alternative way of preparing the profit budget report:

FIGURE 8-10:

ABC DIVISION
Budget Performance Report—January, 1962
(000 omitted)

	Actual	Budget [a]	Favorable/ (Unfavorable) Variance
Sales	$875	$950	$(75)
Variable Costs:			
Material	470	415	(55)
Labor	65	55	(10)
Variable Overhead	90	100	10
Total Variable Costs	$625	$570	$(55)
Contribution	250	380	$(130)
Fixed Overhead	75	75	—
Selling Expense	55	50	(5)
Administrative Expense	30	25	(5)
Total Fixed Costs	$160	$150	$(10)
Profit Performance at Actual			
Volume and Mix	$90	$230	$(140)
Volume Variance			115
Mix Variance			35
Profit Performance from Budget			$10

[a] Budgeted prices and costs at actual sales volume and mix.

The last two performance reports show quite a different story from the first one. Any profit budget performance report must be analyzed in a way similar to these examples if it is to be meaningful to management. In Appendix A an actual budget performance report used by the Westinghouse Electric Corporation has been reproduced.

These examples are necessarily greatly simplified. The problem of calculating mix and volume variance becomes more complicated as the number of products increases. Also, to calculate the variances as described in the text, it is necessary to have standard variable manufacturing costs and to use these costs in the budget. A further complication (to be discussed in the next section) occurs when a company is on a full absorption cost system and the beginning inventory varies from the ending inventory.

The company on a standard direct costing system should have no trouble making the analysis described in this chapter. All of the information necessary to calculate mix and volume variances are available and, with modern computers, the calculation offers no serious problem. Even without a computer, the clerical cost of making these calculations can usually be kept to a reasonable amount. Preprinted forms can reduce the time significantly. If there are a very large number of parts, the high-volume parts can be calculated by part and the remaining parts can be estimated as a single total. In the previous example, for instance, if in addition to Parts A, B, and C there were 1,000 additional parts whose total annual volume was $720,000, the variable costs of these parts could be expressed as a percentage of sales dollars in total as follows:

FIGURE 8-11:

	Total of Parts A, B, and C	Other Parts	Total Profit Budget
		(000 omitted)	
Sales	$7,200	$720	$7,920
Variable Cost:			
Material	3,240	360	3,600
Labor	420	72	492
Variable Overhead	780	144	924
Total Variable Costs	$4,440	$576	$5,016
Contribution	$2,760	$144	$2,904

In preparing actual performance reports, the price, mix and volume variance are calculated for Parts A, B, and C only. The sales of Parts A, B, and C are subtracted from the total sales. The remainder represents the sales of "other parts." Since these are considered to be at budgeted volume, mix, and price, the variable cost allowance is calculated by applying the budgeted percentages to the actual sales. Although not so accurate as making the calculation by part, the method is usually quite satisfactory. If "other parts" represent only 10 per cent to 20 per cent of total sales, the inaccuracies from using this approximation are unlikely to be significant.

If standard costs are not available, the profit budget performance analysis can be approximated by working only with sales volumes. This method is particularly adapted to companies where the variable cost of each product tends to have a consistent relationship to the selling price so that mix variance is unimportant. In this case, the variable costs for the profit budget are developed in total. The per cent of sales of each item of cost is next calculated. When performance reports are prepared, these percentages are applied to the actual sales to obtain the budgeted expense authorization. Here is how a specific calculation is made:

(1) Exclude from actual dollar sales the variance from budgeted prices.

(2) Calculate volume variance as follows (the mix variance is ignored):

(a) Subtract actual sales dollars, adjusted for price variance, from the budgeted sales dollars;

(b) Multiply the amount obtained in (a) by the budgeted per cent of contribution to sales. This is the volume variance.

(3) Calculate the variable cost authorization by multiplying the actual sales dollars, adjusted for price variance, by the budgeted per cent for each item of variable cost:

In the next example the profit budget has been developed as follows:

FIGURE 8-12:

XYZ COMPANY
1962 Profit Budget
(000 omitted)

	Amount	% of Sales
Sales	$600	100%
Variable Costs:		
Material	240	40
Labor	60	10
Variable Overhead	120	20
Total Variable Costs	420	70
Contribution	180	30
Fixed Costs	120	20
Net Profit	$60	10%

If the actual sales in January were $75,000 (of which $5,000 was a favorable price variance) and the profit was $7,000, the budget performance report would be developed in this manner:

FIGURE 8-13:

XYZ COMPANY
Profit Budget Report—January, 1962
(000 omitted)

	Actual	Budget [b]	Favorable/ (Unfavorable) Variance
Sales	$75	$70	$5
Variable Costs:			
Material	30	28	(2)
Labor	8	7	(1)
Variable Overhead	18	14	(4)
Total Variable Cost	$56	$49	$(7)
Contribution	19	21	(2)
Fixed Costs	12	10	(2)
Profit Performance at Actual Volume	$7	$11	$(4)
Volume Variance [a]			6
Profit Performance from Budgeted			2

[a] $(70,000 - 50,000) \times .30 = \$6,000.$
[b] Budgeted prices and costs at actual sales volume.

A variation of this method that takes into consideration differences in sales mix is to develop the profit budget by product line. In this case, the procedure is the same as that described for the ABC Division except that, instead of calculating the budget by units, it is calculated by product line. It is then possible to calculate the profit effect of variances in sales mix among the product lines.

In summary, the method that a company will use for developing the profit budget report will depend on the existence of a standard cost system, the number of products sold, the degree of accuracy desired in the reporting system, and the nature of the sales-cost relationship among its products.

Profit Budget Reports When Sales and Production Volumes Are Different

The analysis described in the previous section assumed that sales volumes and production volumes were equal. This is frequently not the case and, when it is not, the profit budget reporting procedure is complicated. The problem occurs because the variable manufacturing costs are generated by the volume of production, not by the volume of sales. If sales are greater than production, the actual costs of material, direct labor and variable overhead cannot be compared to the costs developed from multiplying standard costs by the sales volume or by multiplying standard cost percentages by sales dollars. The methods for handling this problem will vary depending on the type of cost system employed.

STANDARD DIRECT COSTING

Under a standard direct costing system, there is little problem in adapting the profit budget reporting system. Instead of the variance being reported by material, labor, and variable overhead, they are reported as follows:

FIGURE 8-14:

ABC DIVISION
Budget Performance Report
January, 1962
(000 omitted)

	Actual	Budget	Favorable/ (Unfavorable) Variance
Sales	$875	$950	$(75)
Standard Variable Cost of Sales	570	570	—
Off-Standard Variable Costs	55 [a]		(55)
Total Variable Costs	$625	$570	$(55)
Contribution	250	380	(130)

[a] From schedules 8-5.

(The rest of the report is identical with Figure 8-10.)

The off-standard cost can easily be analyzed and explained on an attached schedule. The format shown in Figure 8-10, however, cannot be used because the off-standard is related to the production volume and the actual variable costs incurred will be different from $625,000 if the production volume is different from the sales volume.

FULL STANDARD COSTING

If full standard costing is used, one more complexity is introduced by the over- or underabsorbed burden. If the production and sales volume are different, the profits under a full absorption system will be different from the profits under a direct costing system. (This was explained in Chapter 5). This difference creates the problem in profit budget reporting and is illustrated by the following example:

Standard Volume .... 100,000 units
Variable Manufacturing Costs (Material,
Direct Labor, and Variable Overhead) .. $2.00 a unit
Fixed Manufacturing Overhead .... $100,000 in total or
$1.00 a unit at standard
volume
Selling Price .... $3.50 a unit

The next schedule shows a comparison of the profits under varying conditions.

FIGURE 8-15:

	Direct Costing	Production 110,000 units	Production 120,000 units	Production 90,000 units
Sales (110,000 units)	$385,000	$385,000	$385,000	$385,000
Cost of Sales	220,000	330,000	330,000	330,000
Fixed Costs	100,000	—	—	—
Gross Profit	$65,000	$55,000	$55,000	$55,000
Over/(Under) Absorbed Overhead	—	10,000	20,000	(10,000)
Net Profit	$65,000	$65,000	$75,000	$45,000

Under a full absorption cost accounting system, the least confusing way of treating this situation for profit budget reporting is to include an item at the bottom of the report called "Profit Effect of Changes in Inventory" and hope that no one in management asks to have it explained. In the first example, the ABC Division, assume that all conditions are the same as given except that the division was on a full absorption system and that January production was as follows:

Part A, 100 units; Part B, 200 units; Part C, 200 units.

The actual profits for January will be changed by this assumption as follows:

FIGURE   8-16A:

ABC DIVISION
Profit Statement—January, 1962
(000 omitted)

Sales	$875.0
Standard Cost of Sales*	682.5
Off-Standard Variable Cost (Figure 8-5)	55.0
Overhead Volume Variance**	(50.0)
Cost of Sales	$687.5
Gross Profit	187.5
Selling & Administrative Expenses	85.0
Net Profit	$102.5

* See Figure 8-16B. ** See Figure 8-16C.

FIGURE   8-16B:

Standard Cost of Sales

Part	Sales	Standard Mfg. Cost Per Unit (a)	Standard Cost of Sales
A	100	$1.05	$105.0
B	200	1.35	270.0
C	150	2.05	307.5
TOTAL			$682.5

(a) Variable cost plus fixed overhead of $.25 per unit.

FIGURE   8-16C:

Overhead Volume Variance
(000 omitted)

Part	Absorbed Overhead *	Budgeted Overhead **	Overhead Volume Variance
A	$45	$45	$—
B	100	75	25
C	90	65	25
	$235	$185	$50

* See Figure 8-16D. ** See Figure 8-16E.

FIGURE   8-16D:

Absorbed Overhead
(000 omitted)

(Calculated as follows: Actual volume × Total standard overhead cost.)

Part	Actual Volume	Standard Overhead Cost Per Unit [a]	Absorbed Overhead
A	100	$.45	$45
B	200	.50	100
C	200	.45	90
			$235

[a] Standard variable overhead + .25 a unit for fixed overhead.

FIGURE   8-16E:

Budgeted Overhead
(000 omitted)

(Calculated as follows: Budgeted fixed costs + [actual volume × Standard variable cost per unit.])

(1) Part	(2) Monthly Fixed Manufacturing Cost	(3) Actual Volume	(4) Variable Manufacturing Overhead Per Unit	(5) Variable Cost at Actual Volume (3 × 4)	Budgeted Cost (2 + 5)
A	$25	100	$.20	$20	$45
B	25	200	.25	50	75
C	25	200	.20	40	65
					$185

The increase in profits from $90,000 to $102,500 is accounted for by the fact that production was higher than sales and consequently inventory has increased. Under a full absorption system, some fixed costs (written off as a period charge under a direct cost system) have been added to inventory. The $12,500 increase in profits can be accounted for as follows:

Part	Production Volume	Sales Volume	Production over/(under) Sales	Fixed Mfg. Cost Per Unit	Increase/ (Decrease) in Profits
			(000 omitted)		
A	100	100	—	$.25	$ —
B	200	200	—	.25	—
C	200	150	50	.25	12.5

In making the profit budget report for January, the same procedure would be followed as shown on Figure 8-9 or Figure 8-10 except that the profit will be $12,500 higher. This will be explained by an item at the bottom called "Profit Effect of Changes in Inventory."

The Profit Budget and the Forecast

In budget administration a distinction should be made between a forecast and a budget. It makes no difference what it is called if everyone understands what it is and uses it accordingly. The danger comes if a company believes that it has a budgetary control system when it really has only a forecast.

A forecast, as the name implies, is merely the best estimate of what will happen; a profit forecast is an estimate of future profit. A budget, on the other hand, is a commitment; a profit budget is a management commitment to attain some given profit level. The confusion between a forecast and a budget occurs because, at the beginning of the period, the two may be the same amount. That is, the manager who prepares a profit budget will normally forecast that he will meet this budget. This is the only point, however, where the two are likely to be the same. The forecast is not reviewed by management except to see if it is realistic and it is not used to evaluate management performance. While the budget stays the same for the entire year, the forecast is changed as soon as more recent data is available.

If a financial projection is not reviewed and approved by management, nor used for evaluating the performance, but is changed periodically, it is not a budget but a forecast. Companies having such a system should not be misled into thinking they have budgetary control.

SUMMARY

A profit budget results when all of the expense budgets are combined with budgeted revenue. The profit budget is used to help evaluate the adequacy of the expense budget, to motivate and evaluate line management in a decentralized organization, and to help in coordinating and planning.

Although the profit budget is essentially an operating budget for a profit center, there are three unique problems in administrating a profit budget system. First, the budgeted sales volume must be considered. Second, the budget proposal for a profit budget is different from an expense budget proposal. Third, pressures develop for short-term profits that should be guarded against.

In reporting actual performance against budget, variances should be explained in terms that can be readily understood by management. In particular, sales volume and mix variance should be segregated from the expense performance part of the report.

CHAPTER NINE

Profit Analysis

This chapter covers two aspects of profit analysis. First, the problem of projecting the effect on profits of a single decision; this is called "differential cost analysis." Second, the graphic representation of the profit pattern of a company; this is called "profit-volume analysis."

DIFFERENTIAL COST ANALYSIS

In making any forward decision, management needs to know the probable effect of this decision on profits. The relevant information is the change in cash flow over the life of the business that will result from taking a specific action (compared with not taking it). The change in cash flow involves two things: the change in revenue and the change in costs. In general, revenue changes from a decision are relatively easy to measure because they are directly related to the projected change in volume. (While the change in volume may be difficult to *estimate*, once estimated, the effect of this change on profits is easy to *measure*.) On the other hand, measuring the cost change resulting from a management decision is frequently quite difficult. This chapter is concerned with the problems of measuring cost changes (or differential costs) resulting from

141

a change in the volume of sales (and, therefore, the volume of production).

Differential Costs Resulting from a Change in Volume

The typical case where differential cost analysis is used involves estimating the cost of producing a given number of additional units or, conversely, the cost savings that will result from not producing a given number of units. The first situation often occurs when a company is given an opportunity to bid on some marginal business. (Normal business is assumed to be unaffected by the outcome of the bid.) Management needs to know the differential cost of producing these units in order to bid intelligently. A similar situation applies when a company is faced with the prospect of losing some business if it does not meet a reduced price level. Management needs to know the cost savings from the reduced volume in order to make a decision. Even though the decision may not be based entirely on the immediate profit effect (for example, the decision may be influenced by the possible effect on other customers), differential costs are necessary before management can make a rational decision.

ESTIMATING DIFFERENTIAL COST

It is important to realize that the relationship of cost to volume is not constant, but is different under different conditions. Variable costs calculated for one purpose are sometimes used for another. This can be dangerous because in a given company at a given time the variability of a cost will be affected by at least three factors: (1) the degree of the change in volume; (2) the permanency of the change; and (3) the volume of production at the time of the change. Needless to say, the relationship of cost to volume can be different for different companies and different for the same company at different times. In calculating differential costs, therefore, *the most accurate way is to estimate the change in cash flow that will occur in the specific situation being studied.*

Clearly, a special study is not always practicable or necessary. Sometimes the amount of the costs in question are so small that a significant error in projecting their variability would not affect the decision. (As a practical matter, semivariable manufacturing expenses and certain selling expenses are frequently the only ones in question; other expenses are either variable or fixed.) Sometimes the nature of the study is such that the other factors are subject to a wide range of uncertainty; under this condition, a detailed study of the variable costs may only add meaningless accuracy. In other cases, there may not be time to make a detailed study. In the absence of a detailed study, it is usual to use the flexible budget relationship of cost to volume for estimating the differential overhead cost. This is not necessarily wrong and is sometimes the only practical action. There is, however, a danger that should be considered. The variable costs, as calculated for use in a flexible budget system, normally provide for the minimum amount of variability that is likely to be experienced.

FACTORS THAT AFFECT DIFFERENTIAL COSTS

As stated, there are three important factors that can affect the variability of an overhead cost. Their effect should be considered carefully before using the flexible budget relationship for estimating differential costs.

Degree of change. In calculating the effect on costs of a change in volume, the degree of change is perhaps the most important. If volume were to double, for example, *all* costs may be variable. This would be true if a new plant had to be built. As a matter of fact, costs may increase *in excess* of total accounted costs if the new plant were more expensive than the old. If, however, an increase in volume is relatively small, it may be handled without additional equipment. In this case, the variable costs will generally be considerably less than the total costs. *The flexible budget equation is designed to measure the cost effect of changes in volume within a limited area around standard volume.*

Permanency of change. If a change in volume is permanent, it usually has a greater impact on costs than if it were temporary. For example, it may be possible to operate for short periods of time at a higher volume without adding more supervision. If the change is permanent, it may be necessary to increase supervisory costs proportionately to the increase in volume. The same is true of a reduction in volume. It may not be desirable to reduce supervisory personnel for a temporary reduction in volume. If the reduction was permanent, however, in time supervisory personnel would be reduced with the lower volume of operations.

Even the amount of equipment and, consequently, depreciation and taxes, may increase if a change is permanent. For instance, a short-term change may be handled on present equipment. If the change is permanent, however, an increase in equipment may occur when the old equipment is replaced.

The flexible budget equation is designed to measure the cost effect of temporary changes.

Existing volume of production. When flexible budgets were discussed, it was pointed out that the variable cost ratio was a linear approximation of that part of the cost-volume curve in the range near standard volume. The relationship of cost to volume is almost always curvilinear rather than linear and, by definition, the slope of a curve is different at different points. This is another way of saying that the ratio of cost to volume (the variable cost ratio) will be different at different volumes. This is evident when the cost of an additional 1,000 units (say 10 per cent of standard volume) is estimated. If the plant is operating at capacity, the differential cost of the 1,000 units will be quite different from the costs that would result if it is operating at 50 per cent of capacity.

It is not only at capacity that the variable cost ratio will change. Most production processes have points where costs will increase in steps; adding a second shift is an example of such a step. In estimating variable costs, therefore, it is important to consider the possibility of having such a step change.

FLEXIBLE BUDGETS AS AN ESTIMATE OF DIFFERENTIAL COST

Variable costs, as calculated for use in a flexible budget system, are estimated to reflect temporary changes over a relatively small range of production, at a range near standard volume. For this reason they usually provide for a smaller degree of variability than would normally be experienced in many situations requiring differential costs. This does not mean that the overhead budget relationship cannot be used in projecting future costs in, for example, a decision to make a bid on some marginal business. It does mean, however, that it should be used *with care*. The budget relationship between costs and volume should be a reasonable basis for the particular purpose for which it is being used.

Closing a Plant

In instances where a company is faced with the necessity of selling its products below full costs, it is appropriate to consider the possibility of closing down a plant. Many costs that are fixed above this point can be eliminated when a plant is closed. In many cases, all costs except depreciation and taxes can be eliminated. If the plant can be sold, even these expenses may be eliminated.

Management is sometimes misled into keeping a plant open that should be closed because several decisions have been made independently. For example, several sales may have been made at more than variable costs (for a going plant) but less than full costs. Each individual sale appeared to make a contribution to fixed overhead and, therefore, seemed to be the correct decision. The differential costs used in making each decision were based on the fact that the plan was in operation and only the cost of producing the additional units were considered. If all of these decisions had been made at the same time, however, it might be evident that money would be saved by closing down the entire plant.

Closing a plant is a drastic action and often management would not want to do it even though it were temporarily economical. The problems of starting up again when business becomes better or a reluctance to create dislocation problems among its employees might well be the determining factor. Even in this case, management needs to know how much it is going to cost to stay in business. This cost is the difference between the cash flow if the plant is kept open and the cash flow if the plant is closed.

Differential Costs at Capacity

When a plant is working at capacity, the differential cost problem is quite different from when the plant is working at less than capacity. In the latter, the problem is to estimate the change in costs that is expected to result from a specific change in volume. When the plant is at capacity, however, these figures are frequently meaningless. At capacity, the alternative might not be whether to *add* a given number of units of a product but whether to *substitute* a given number of units of one product for another.

For example, assume that Plant X is currently working at capacity. If the manager is given an opportunity for additional business, he may be able to do one of two things:

(1) Produce the additional units on an overtime basis; or

(2) Substitute the additional units for some less profitable business.

The decision depends upon which alternative provides the greatest amount of cash flow.

In calculating profitability when production is below capacity, the amount of contribution *per unit* is the relevant figure. At capacity, however, the relevant figure is *contribution per unit of capacity*. The unit of capacity is determined by the limiting production factor. If capacity is limited by machine hours, the most profitable product is the one that provides the greatest contribution per machine hour. When the plant is working at capacity, for example, the manager can maximize his profits by reducing the production of the products that give the smallest contribution per machine hour while increasing the production on the products that provide the greatest contribution per machine hour.

In practical business situations, it is sometimes difficult to define capacity with any degree of precision or even to decide exactly what the limiting production factors are. The necessity of line balancing, the composition of product mix, the differences in the different departments all make this a complex problem. The important point to be remembered, however, is that different cost figures are required for decision-making when production is limited by ability to produce rather than sales orders.

Wearing Out a Production Line

The contribution concept is frequently misused as a result of assuming that a production line (or plant) can be worn out. The typical situation occurs under the following conditions: a product is losing money; an analysis shows that the price is above the variable cost of production; there appears to be little likelihood of the price increasing or the costs decreasing. In this situation, management is faced with the problem of deciding whether or not to get out of the business. Sometimes the decision is made to stay in the business until the present equipment "wears out." The theory is that this will be a means of recovering, through depreciation, part of the investment in the equipment. This decision would be correct except for one fallacy: a production line rarely wears out. It must generally be maintained and partially replaced each year. At the end of ten years, the equipment will probably be in as good condition as it is today. In the meantime, replacements may have equaled the so-called "sunk" depreciation costs.

Contribution is a perfectly good basis for a short-run decision but it can be questionable for a long-run decision. In the example above, if it were a question of a temporarily depressed price, the decision to stay in business until the selling price again became higher should be made on the basis of contribution. For long-run decisions, however, it is necessary to take into account the fact that the differential costs are usually higher when considering the long run. In particular, production equipment is usually not like Oliver Wendell Holmes' celebrated "one-horse shay" that lasted for 100 years and collapsed into a heap of dust on its 100th birthday.

Accounting for Differential Costs

It has been demonstrated that the differential cost of producing one unit of a product will be different under different circumstances. It is not possible, therefore, to have the accounting system provide differential costs on a routine basis. Direct costing systems provide an approximation of short-term differential costs but by no means can these costs be used to make all decisions. Although the cost accounting system cannot provide differential costs regularly, it should provide information that will facilitate the calculation of differential costs as a special study. This usually involves providing the kind of historical cost data that is useful for estimating the costs of forward decisions.

Using an Asset Already Owned

In most cases, the calculation of differential costs involves estimating the out-of-pocket costs of production in a given situation. A more complex problem involves using in a proposed project an asset already owned (and, therefore, requiring no cash outlay). This section describes some of the possible ramifications of this problem.

If, for example, the proposal is to expand the production of a product by adding a new production line occupying 5,000 square feet of plant space currently idle, the question is how much, if anything, is the differential cost of the floor space? Although the answer to this question will depend on the individual circumstances, the following generalizations may be used as guides in making this decision:

1. The accounting allocation for the cost of the building depreciation, taxes, and so forth, per square foot of floor space is irrelevant. It would represent the differential cost value only by coincidence.

2. If there are other immediate uses for the space, the differential cost of the space is equal to the cost of the most expensive alternative. For example, if the space could be used to warehouse inventory and because of using this space for the new production line, warehouse space in an outside warehouse must be rented, the differential cost of the space is equal to the cost of the outside warehousing.

   In making the calculation, the differential cost of the floor space is equal to all of the cost differences between storing the inventory in the space in question and storing the inventory in an outside warehouse. If there is a cost penalty because of extra handling in the outside warehouse, this is added to the rental charge of the outside warehouse space.

   In calculating the differential cost of space where there is an alternative use, it is important to calculate the total effect on the costs to the company of devoting this space to the proposed use, rather than the alternative use. This may mean several changes. If the alternative to putting in the new line is to produce Product A in this area and use the area now occupied by Product A to store finished goods now being stored in a rental warehouse, the differential cost of the space is the cost of the outside warehousing plus the savings in costs from having Product A produced in the new area.

3. If there are no uses for the floor space during the period when the decision is to be in effect, then it has no differential cost. For

changes that will be completed in a relatively short period of time, it is usually easy to decide whether or not there are alternative uses. If, however, the change will be in effect on a long-term basis, determining whether or not there are alternative uses for the floor space may be difficult. It would be unusual if some alternative use could not be found eventually for almost any floor space. To treat this floor space as having no differential cost is, therefore, incorrect. When the asset has no immediate alternative use, but the decision covers a long period of time, the following generalizations apply:

a. Decide if the inclusion of a maximum reasonable differential cost for the floor space can be a critical factor (that is, affect the decision). If it cannot affect the decision, ignore it.

b. If the possible amount of differential cost is large enough to affect the decision, estimate: (1) the alternative use of the floor space; (2) the value of this alternative use (as described by [2] above); and (3) the timing of this alternative use. (Since there is no immediate use, the alternative must be sometime in the future.) The differential cost of the floor space is the present value of the annual costs from not having the floor space available for its alternative use in the future. This means that the further in the future that the alternative use is, the less important it will be. (This amount is *added* to the investment.)

Although the use of present value theory in making decisions is outside the scope of this book, a discussion of differential cost analysis is incomplete without at least mentioning it. When the decision affects a major asset for a long period of time, the analysis must consider the present value of alternative uses. For example, a company has an idle plant. There is a proposal to use that plant immediately to produce Product A; within three years, it is estimated that a more profitable use of the plant will be available. The question is whether to use the plant *now* for the less profitable item or hold it idle for three years and then produce the more profitable item. (A change-over is assumed to be uneconomical at the end of three years.) The question can be answered by determining the present value of three cash flows: (1) from producing Product A in the old plant; (2) from producing the alternative product in the old plant, beginning three years from now; and (3) from producing the alternative product in the best available alternative plant, with Product A assumed to occupy the present plant.

The use of discounted cash flow in decision-making is a complex subject that requires considerable study in itself. Chapter 18 of *Management Accounting: Text and Cases,* by Robert N. Anthony has an excellent description of the principles and procedures of present value analysis. The purpose of this section is not to explain present value and discounted cash flow concepts but to point out that they can be applicable to certain problems in differential cost analyses.

To summarize, in general, differential cost analysis involves only costs that can be measured by direct cash outflow. In some cases, however, indirect cash flow must be reflected in differential costs. The most common example of this situation results from using an available asset. If the asset has alternative uses, the differential cost of the asset is its value in the most favorable alternative use. If it has no alternative use during the period affected by the decision, it has no differential cost. If the decision will be in effect a long period of time, and if the asset is a general purpose one, the possibility of future use must be considered. (Only be concerned about this, however, if the amount is material enough to affect the decision.) In analyzing future use, the analysis should take into account the fact that a dollar today is worth more than a dollar in the future. (The alternative use can be safely ignored if it is far enough into the future.) Where the asset is large and the alternative future uses are more profitable than present uses, a discounted cash flow analysis is required.

PROFIT-VOLUME ANALYSIS

Perhaps the most commonly used chart in profit analysis is the profit-volume chart or the breakeven chart. These charts have two basic forms with an almost infinite number of variations. In this part of the chapter, the construction and the uses of the profit-volume and breakeven charts are explained.

The two basic forms are demonstrated below. The first one is usually called a "breakeven chart" and the second is usually called a "profit-volume chart." Actually, both charts have the same general purposes:

Construction of Breakeven and Profit-Volume Charts

The techniques described in Chapter 6 for developing flexible manufacturing overhead budgets may be used in developing breakeven charts or profit-volume charts. The principal difference is that a breakeven chart applies to an entire business, including all costs as well as revenues.

USING THE PROFIT BUDGET RELATIONSHIP

Where a company has already prepared a profit budget that separates the fixed and variable costs, a breakeven chart and profit-volume chart is very easy to develop. Plot budgeted profits at any two volumes

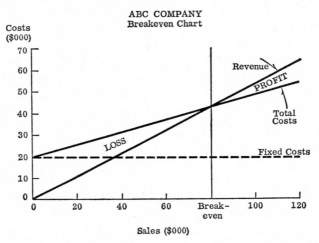

(usually zero and standard volume) on a chart and connect them with a straight line. This is the company's profit-volume line. A breakeven chart is equally easy except that it is necessary to plot three lines: fixed cost, variable costs and revenues.

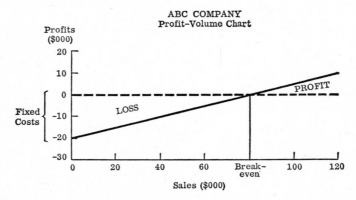

The fixed cost line is, of course, a horizontal line. (Remember that it includes *all* fixed costs, not just fixed overhead.) The variable cost lines and the revenue line can be determined by plotting the total revenue and total variable cost at standard volume; the revenue line is drawn from the zero point (the intersection of the *x* and *y* axes) through the plotted point at standard volume; the variable cost line is drawn from the point where the fixed cost line intersects the y axis to the plotted point of total cost at standard volume.

If there is no profit budget (or the profit budget does not separate the fixed and variable costs) the following methods can be used for constructing a profit-volume or breakeven chart.

FITTING A LINE TO HISTORICAL DATA

This method is basically the same as that used to determine the variability of manufacturing overhead costs. Actual profits are plotted against volumes on the chart and a line is fitted to the plot points either by sight or by the method of least squares (see Appendix B). A breakeven chart can be made by plotting total costs against volume and adding a revenue line. For example, the monthly income statements for the ABC Company show the following information:

Month	Sales	Costs	Profits/(Loss)
		(000 omitted)	
January	$1,000	$900	$100
February	1,300	1,100	200
March	1,400	1,200	200
April	500	650	(150)
May	600	700	(100)
June	1,200	1,000	200
July	900	900	—
August	800	850	(50)
September	1,400	1,100	300
October	700	650	50
November	1,200	1,100	100
December	700	700	—

A profit-volume chart can be developed as follows (the line is fitted by sight):

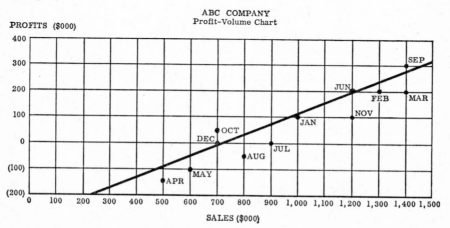

ABC COMPANY
Profit-Volume Chart

A breakeven chart would be developed as follows:

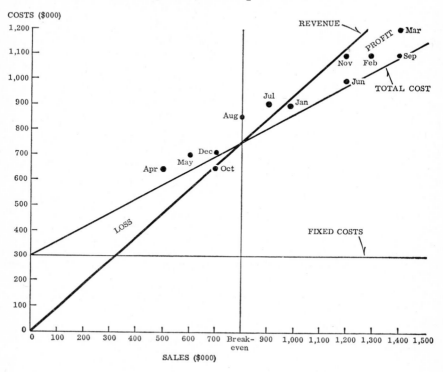

In using historical data to develop a breakeven or profit-volume chart, two possible distortions must be avoided:

1. The shorter the period of time covered by the profit amount, the relatively greater will be the random fluctuations resulting from the inherent inaccuracies of profit measurement. For example, the amount of inventory is an important factor in profit determination. In a monthly income statement, inventories are frequently only roughly approximated; yet, an error in the amount of inventory will have twelve times the relative effect on monthly profits as the same mistake will have on the annual profits. (Usually, also, the annual inventory is much more carefully calculated.)

2. If the historical information covers a relatively large period of time, significant changes in the breakeven point may be occurring during the period. Fitting a line to this date will not give the current profit-volume line. If annual profits are plotted over a period of five years during which a company was expanding, it might show an excellent fit on a profit-volume chart. This does not mean that profits will drop along this

line when volume drops. (Facilities and fixed costs have probably increased proportionately with sales volume.) This point can be demonstrated by a simple, though extreme, example. Suppose a company employed a chemical processing technique that was characterized by having costs that are 100 per cent fixed. A plant costs $100,000 a year to operate and could produce a maximum of 100,000 pounds, selling at $1.50 a pound. As sales increased beyond the capacity of the current plant, additional plants are added. Assume that sales, costs, and profits are as follows:

Year	Sales Pounds	Sales Dollars	Costs	Profits	Number of Plants in Operation
1955	75,000	112,500	$100,000	$12,500	1
1956	100,000	150,000	100,000	50,000	1
1957	150,000	225,000	200,000	25,000	2
1958	220,000	330,000	300,000	30,000	3
1959	250,000	375,000	300,000	75,000	3

A profit-volume chart would look somewhat as follows:

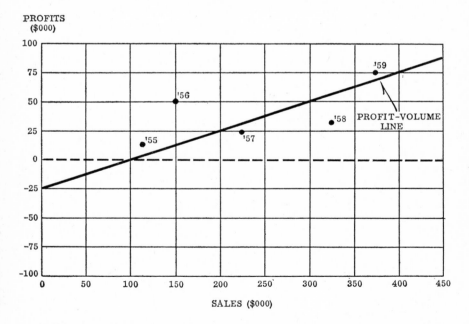

Although there are several other possible ways to fit the line (including one that shows no fixed costs at zero volume) all will include some variability. In fact, the fixed costs are $300,000 and, since there are no variable costs, the breakeven point is at a $300,000 sales volume. This conclusion would never be drawn from the profit-volume chart above because this chart reflects the changes in fixed costs over the years. Although the example is extreme, there will be the same type of distortion (although less in magnitude) any time profit-volume data is plotted covering a period of time when the company has been changing in size.

PLOTTING TWO POINTS

Other methods for developing a breakeven or profit-volume chart are similar to those described in Chapter 6 for developing flexible budget ratios. Consequently, these methods will be described only briefly here. The methods involve obtaining two points on the chart and drawing a straight line between them. The two points may be derived from analysis or from historical data. A frequent method is to calculate profit at zero volume and standard volume and connect these two points with a line. Another common method is to calculate profits at 90 per cent and 110 per cent (or some other percentages such as 80 per cent and 120 per cent) of standard volume and connect these points with a line. Another method is to take the profits at the highest and lowest volumes experienced during the past year and connect these points with a line. (When this is done, it is usual to adjust both profit amounts for unusual items.) The principal disadvantage of using only two points is that a distortion in either point can affect the line seriously.

Uses of Profit-Volume and Breakeven Charts

The profit-volume or breakeven chart is a simple graphic presentation of the relationship of profit to volume. These charts are easy for management to understand and use. Their principal advantages are as follows:

1. They furnish a simple evaluation of current profit levels. Actual profits are plotted on the profit-volume chart and management can see at a glance whether the level is better or worse than expected at the actual volume of operations. In other words, they show the profit performance adjusted for volume.

2. They provide management with a handy tool for calculating the effect of planned volume changes quickly.

3. They demonstrate graphically the approximate sales volume at which the company will lose money. If several breakeven points for different periods of time are plotted on the same chart, it shows graphically the changes in the breakeven points, the changes in the fixed costs, and the changes in contribution per sales dollar. (I have seen a simple profit-

volume chart prove to management why profits had been steadily deterio-
rating over the past several years.)

LIMITATIONS OF PROFIT-VOLUME AND BREAKEVEN CHARTS

Although profit-volume and breakeven charts are a useful tool to
management, they will by no means solve problems in themselves. The
best they can do is to help management diagnose a problem. All of the
information shown on a profit-volume chart is frequently available in
tabular form on an accounting report. The profit-volume chart merely
presents this information in a more meaningful manner. These charts
have several weaknesses of which the user should be aware. Their principal limitations are as follows:

1. Unless the chart includes only one product, the profit-volume
chart assumes a constant mix. Actual profits can vary from the profit-
volume line because proportionately more of one product was sold than
was assumed in developing the profit-volume chart. (This can also be
a problem in developing a profit-volume chart from historical data.)

2. The profit-volume line is a linear approximation of a curvilinear
function. The further away actual volume is from the volumes used to
develop the line, the less accurate will be this approximation.

3. Many factors can cause actual profits to be different from that
indicated by the profit-volume line, yet the chart does not show the reasons for variance. For example, actual profits can be different from those
indicated in the chart because prices changed, mix changed or cost
changed. Differences also occur because the profit-volume line only ap-
proximates the profit-volume relationship. The chart does not indicate in
any way what caused the variances; worse offsetting variances will never
be detected.

4. Like all charts, the profit-volume chart shows a limited amount
of information. All of the information shown on a profit-volume chart
will usually occupy only a portion of an 8½ by 11-inch report.

CHAPTER TEN

Two Special Control Techniques

The purpose of this chapter is to describe two special control techniques. The term "special" is used because these techniques are not applicable to all businesses but, rather, are useful only in particular cases. The two techniques involve the control of purchased material costs and the development of standard selling prices. These techniques are described in this book because they are unusual applications of cost accounting methods. Although not widely used in industry today, they are capable of providing management with more useful information than that obtained from some of the more traditional cost accounting applications. In the author's opinion, many businesses could employ these techniques to good advantage.

CONTROL OF PURCHASED MATERIAL COSTS

In many businesses, purchased materials are by far the largest item of expense; yet frequently less effort is directed toward controlling these expenses than toward any other item on the income statement. To be sure, in many instances, material costs cannot be influenced by the individual business and, to this extent, it is foolish to establish an elaborate set of controls. There are, however, many cases where material costs are subject to at least partial control by the purchaser. The purpose of this section of the chapter is to describe methods for controlling purchased material costs under these circumstances.

Standard Costs and Material Cost Control

Many accountants believe that a standard cost system always will provide a control over material prices. This is not true at all. *The typical standard cost system will do nothing more than keep track of price changes that occur during the year.* (Standard costs may be useful, however, in controlling material usage.)

The typical standard cost system establishes standard material prices at current levels, adjusted for expected changes during the coming year. In no way do these standards indicate what the material should cost, as in the case of direct labor and overhead. An off-standard material price variance means only that prices are different from those that were anticipated. A standard cost report does not inform management whether the purchasing department's performance is good or bad. (A favorable variance is not necessarily good; perhaps prices should have been reduced more than they were.)

A danger to the use of material cost standards is that frequently these standards are interpreted to be engineered standards because variances from these prices are reflected in the budget performance report. That is, a price less than standard is treated as good performance; a price greater than standard is treated as poor performance. Because the standard prices are merely forward estimates of costs, variations do not represent good or bad performance.

Standard material costs are useful in forward planning and establishing standard prices (to be discussed in the next part of the chapter) and should be used for these purposes only. If a system of material cost control and performance evaluation is required (and frequently it is not) other methods, such as these described in this chapter, are necessary.

Situations Requiring Material Cost Controls

A formal material cost control system is usually required under the following conditions:

1. Material costs can be influenced by the purchaser. This occurs when:

   (a) The buyer and the seller negotiate the price. This happens most frequently on differentiated products (that is, designed for a specific purpose) because there are no standard price lists.

(With general purpose products, on the other hand, the prices
are usually set by catalogue and are traditionally on a take-it-
or-leave-it basis so that the purchaser has no control over the
price that he pays.)

(b) Material *costs* can be influenced through judicious buying. This
happens when:

(i) market prices vary significantly during the year; and

(ii) a sufficiently large inventory can be maintained to take
advantage of low prices.

2. Controllable material costs are an important part of the costs of
production.

3. The business is large enough and complex enough so that management cannot keep a day-to-day control on the purchasing activity by
personal observation.

Purchased Material Control System—Differentiated Products

The system for controlling the cost of purchased parts is based on
establishing a standard price for each part on a "control list." The control
list consists of those parts that have sufficiently large potential savings to
make it worthwhile to establish a control over them.

The standard price for a purchased part is calculated by estimating
how much it *should* cost an efficient producer to manufacture the part
and then adding a normal profit to this cost. The estimate must frequently
be fairly broad because the purchaser will not have access to detailed
production records. In most instances, material and labor are estimated
from processing sheets. Overhead is usually expressed as a percentage of
direct labor. This percentage is based on an estimate of the overhead rate
applicable to the type of production process assumed in estimating the
direct labor. (Incidentally, this is frequently the most difficult factor to
estimate accurately.) A percentage is then added to cover selling and
administrative expenses and profit.

A typical material cost control system operates as follows:

1. A list of control parts is established. The inclusion of an item on
the list depends upon the degree of control the purchaser has over
the price he pays and the volume of the purchases (in other words,
the potential cost savings available). The parts are normally listed
in order of the potential cost savings.

2. A standard price for each item on the control list is established.
As stated, this price is based on an estimate of the production
cost plus a reasonable profit allowance.

3. The standard initial cost estimates are reviewed with the buyer
of each part and a standard price that is acceptable to the buyer

is agreed upon. Minor deviations between standard and actual are eliminated at this point. For example, if the standard price of a part turned out to be $2.10 and the actual price was $2.13, the standard price would usually be adjusted to $2.13.

4. A monthly report is prepared, by buyer, showing the profit effect of the variances of actual prices from standard.

5. The standards are adjusted periodically to reflect changes in the design of the part and changes in the general level of raw material costs and wage rates.

6. A periodic report (monthly or quarterly) is prepared showing changes in the actual cost of materials over the period. These changes are broken down by cause, as follows:

(a) Economic changes. (Those resulting from over-all changes in raw material costs and wage rates.)

(b) Design changes. (Those resulting from changes in the design of the product.)

(c) Negotiated changes. (Those not caused by either economic or design changes.)

This report can be applied to the control items only or to all items. The base price is the price at the beginning of the period. The economic effect of the price change can be approximated by multiplying the price change by 50 per cent of the volume of the period. (Assume that, on an average, all changes will be made in the middle of the period.)

The advantages of this system are: (1) it provides the buyer with an objective guide to the adequacy of the prices being paid for the parts that he is responsible for buying; (2) it gives the buyer a better basis for negotiation; (3) it provides a general method of evaluating the effectiveness of the buyer; (4) it focuses management's attention on the material cost problems; (5) it indicates possible parts to start producing; (6) it is useful in planning because it helps to provide an approximation of the possible direction of future material costs.

Its disadvantages are: (1) it can be expensive to operate, since it may require the development of a purchase analysis department; and (2) some of the standard purchase material costs may be inaccurate.

The question to be decided is whether the savings from a material cost control system will be sufficiently large to more than offset the cost of the system. (Remember, however, that the system can be applied to any number of parts and the critical problem is usually "where to stop" not "whether to start.")

The purchased standards are not generally used in the cost accounting system. Where a standard cost system is in effect, the standard material costs would continue to be based on forecast material prices.

Purchased Material Control System—Common Products

Where a company purchases products that are common to an industry, there is little point in calculating a standard price. There is nothing that a buyer can do even if armed with a detailed cost analysis proving the purchase price is too high. Also, included in this group are raw materials whose prices are generally not directly related to production costs in any event. The average company can minimize the cost of these materials only through judicious buying. That is, buying when the prices are low and placing any excess stock into inventory. The most effective buyer will minimize the total cost of purchasing and warehousing. The problem in evaluation is to determine how good a job has been done. One way is to recalculate, at the end of each year (or other appropriate period), what the optimum performance would have been with perfect foresight, but with all other restraints as they actually existed. Depending on the number and complexity of these restraints, the mathematical formulation of the optimum might be fairly complex but still practical using modern operations research techniques.

The optimum compared with the actual gives an indication of performance. The performance standard will have to be developed from experience because, in the beginning, only a vague idea exists of what constitutes good performance.

The advantages of such a control system are: (1) it will provide a motivation to the buyer to minimize total costs because he will know that errors in judgment will be reflected in his performance; (2) it will provide management with a general evaluation of performance (rough as it is, it is better than nothing); (3) it may demonstrate to both the buyer and management the effectiveness of certain techniques in buying and inventory control.

The disadvantages are: (1) the purchasing people will oppose it (at least initially) on the grounds that it is unfair and provides little evaluation of their performance; (2) the method (particularly the mathematical formulation) is new and may be difficult for operating management to understand; (3) it is only a rough indication of performance and in some cases might be unreliable; (4) it may be expensive to develop.

In all control systems, the advantages of a control technique must more than offset the disadvantages. In this case, the amount of purchases, the possible savings from optimizing the cost of purchasing and warehousing, and the possible improvement over present performance will decide whether it would be worthwhile to install the kind of system described here. (If it will not result in lower costs, clearly it is not worth spending any money to install.) Starting the program by experimenting with one or two products may be advantageous.

Summary

Purchased materials represent the largest single item of cost in many companies; yet little is done to control these costs in most accounting and control systems. In many cases, little can be done to change material costs and, therefore, there is no point in establishing sophisticated control techniques. If material cost controls are required, however, techniques similar to those described in this part of the chapter should be used. (Remember that the typical standard cost system offers only nominal control of material costs.) The decision as to whether these techniques should be employed will depend upon the estimated cost savings compared to the cost of operating the control system.

THE STANDARD SELLING PRICE

In many companies the most important use of cost accounting data is in revenue control. This section of the chapter describes a system for using cost information to assist management in evaluating selling prices. This system involves calculating a standard selling price for all major items sold and preparing a monthly or quarterly report comparing actual selling prices to these standards.

The idea of a standard selling price is not new. General Motors Corporation used this concept as early as the 1920's.[1] Standard prices for revenue control do not seem to have been adopted extensively outside of the automotive industry. The concept does, however, have application to any business where prices are not determined entirely by competition. As long as there is any differentiation in product or service, there must be an opportunity (even though the range may be small) for price differentiation. The purpose of the standard price is to provide management with information, not available from traditional cost accounting reports, upon which to base selling price decisions. Such information is designed to focus managment's attention on the products that appear to be underpriced.

Developing Standard Prices

In establishing a standard price, the objective is to estimate the price that would be charged by a normal, efficient producer. One common way of doing this is to estimate the cost of producing the part (in an efficient manner but on present facilities) and add a normal profit to this cost. This

[1] See Albert Bradley's article in the January, 1927, N.A.C.A. Bulletin.

calculation will be similar to that for estimating standard material prices. In the case of the standard selling price, however, detailed cost and processing information is available. Standard costs generally provide an excellent basis for the estimate of production costs. If the standard cost includes some unusual factor to provide for local conditions, eventually this should be eliminated. To begin with, unusual conditions can be ignored because they will become evident when actual selling prices are compared to the standard and the causes of the variances analyzed.

The fixed cost and profit element of the standard price should be related to the investment in the facilities required to produce the part. This calculation can be simplified by allocating fixed costs and assets to product lines and calculating the fixed cost and profit requirements for all items in the line as a percentage of variable cost. The purpose is not to have an exact relationship between investment and profit requirement but an approximate one. The total profit for all product lines should provide an adequate profit for the business, with efficiency assumed to equal that reflected in the standard costs. An example of such a calculation is as follows:

FIGURE   10-1:

DFG   COMPANY
1962 Profit Budget
(000 omitted)

Sales	$25,000
Variable Costs	
Material	8,000
Labor	4,000
Variable Overhead	4,000
Total Variable Costs	$16,000
Contribution	$9,000
Fixed Costs:	
Fixed Overhead	$4,000
Selling Expense	1,000
Administrative Expense	1,000
Total Fixed Costs	$6,000
Net Profit	$3,000
Working Capital	$5,000
Fixed Assets	10,000
Total Investment	$15,000

The next step is to break down the profit budget by product line and to calculate the standard percentage of variable costs that will be required to cover fixed costs and profits. If a return on investment of

25 per cent before taxes is considered reasonable for this type of operation, the calculation might be as follows:

FIGURE 10-2:

DFG COMPANY
Profit Requirements by Product Line
(000 omitted)

	Product Line A	Product Line B	Product Line C	Total Company
Variable Costs:				
Material	$4,000	$2,000	$2,000	$8,000
Labor	1,000	2,000	1,000	4,000
Variable Overhead	1,000	2,000	1,000	4,000
Total Variable Costs	$6,000	$6,000	$4,000	$16,000
Fixed Costs:				
Fixed Overhead	1,000	1,000	2,000	4,000
Selling Expense	500	400	100	1,000
Administrative Expense	400	300	300	1,000
Total Fixed Costs	$1,900	$1,700	$2,400	$6,000
Investment:				
Working Capital	$2,500	$1,250	$1,250	$5,000
Fixed Assets	2,500	2,500	5,000	10,000
TOTAL	$5,000	$3,750	$6,250	$15,000
25% of Investment	$1,250	$938	$1,562	$3,750
Fixed Costs	1,900	1,700	2,400	6,000
Total Fixed Costs and Profits	$3,150	$2,638	$3,962	$9,750
Fixed Costs and Profits ÷ Variable Costs	53%	44%	99%	

(The allocations to product line would be made using the techniques described in Chapter 3. Working capital is allocated to product line on the basis of variable costs.)

Standard prices of three representative items are calculated as follows:

Item	Variable Cost	Fixed Cost and Profit	Standard Price
Product Line A, Item 361	$1.50	$.80	$2.30
Product Line B, Item 42	1.00	.44	1.44
Product Line C, Item 13	3.00	2.97	5.97

There are many techniques and short cuts for calculating standard prices. For example, a single percentage for an entire plant is satisfactory if the variable costs are representative of the investment in fixed equipment dedicated to each of the product lines. Any method will be satisfactory as long as: (1) the variable costs are representative of a reasonably efficient operation, consistent among products; and (2) the fixed costs and profit on investment approximate the fixed costs and assets dedicated to the products when reasonable allocation techniques are used.

The procedure described in this section presupposes a standard cost system. Where standard costs are not available, it is usually possible to estimate efficient production costs for major products and include only these major products on a standard price report. (Remember that, in the typical business, a small number of products accounts for a large proportion of the total sales.)

The Standard Price Report

The standard price report is issued either monthly, quarterly, semiannually or annually. The time period is dependent upon the pricing action that can be taken. If monthly pricing action is appropriate, then monthly reports should be provided. Remember, however, that much of the information provided by this report is designed to indicate to management where pricing problems exist. These problems will not usually be solved each month, with a new set of problems occurring the following month. Rather, some may never be solved and others, only after a period of years. Some problems, of course, can be corrected quickly. In general then, quarterly or even semiannual reports will prove to be sufficient.

Although the format of the report can take many forms, below is a suggested format:

DFG COMPANY
Report of Actual Prices vs. Standard Prices
Quarter Ending March 31, 1962

Part Number	Actual Volume of Sales	Actual Price	Standard Price	Actual over/(under) Standard	Profit Effect of Prices over/(under) Standard
A361	$200,000	$2.00	$2.30	$(.30)	$(30,000)
B 42	105,000	1.40	1.44	(.04)	(3,000)
C 13	100,000	6.10	5.97	.13	2,200
All other	10,000				800
TOTAL	$415,000				$(30,000)

(In an actual business situation, of course, a much larger number of parts would be shown.)

In general, items should be listed in the order of their price deficiency. At some point, lower volume parts must be grouped for presentation to management; otherwise, the report might include pages of relatively meaningless statistics. (A large number of low-volume parts will usually account for only a small proportion of the total business.)

Who Should Prepare a Standard Price Report?

A standard price report is useful in a business having the following characteristics:

1. The business is large enough and complex enough for management to require a formal revenue report. The only purpose of this report is to provide management with certain information relative to pricing. The report will be useless if management already has a day-to-day knowledge of the information included on the report.

2. Revenue action is possible. (Revenue action includes changing prices, product mix or design.) Many people mistake the opportunity for restricted revenue action as no opportunity for revenue action. If the product or service is differentiated, or if sales mix can be influenced at all, there is usually some room for revenue action. The question is whether the range of revenue action is sufficient to warrant instituting a standard price report. In companies that have a standard cost system, the additional cost of such a report may be quite small. In small business, however, the limited room for revenue action, the lack of accounting information, and the possible savings from independent action may make a standard price report impracticable.

Advantage of a Standard Price Report

The principal advantage of the standard price report is that it forces management to consider possible action with respect to products whose profits are significantly out of line. Somewhat the same information is provided to management by the traditional product-line profit statement. The problem with traditional profit reports, however, is that cost and volume factors tend to obscure revenue factors. For example, the low volume of sales and off-standard costs can contribute to the low profit. The standard price report, on the other hand, is not affected by cost inefficiencies and volume fluctuations. The off-standard prices must result from some other causes such as: temporarily depressed prices from excess supply; permanently depressed price from excess capacity in the industry; products of higher quality or more expensive design than competitors'; standard cost out of line with competitors' costs; an economic cost disadvantage (such as labor rates or geographical location).

It is important that the reason for each major price deficiency be analyzed and a cause assigned, if possible. The first step is to examine the standard price buildup to see if any unusual conditions exist in the company that could cause the variance. (Ignore minor deviations because they probably result from inherent inaccuracies of the estimate.) Once it has been decided that the price estimates are accurate, the price deficiency must be due to one of the causes mentioned in the previous paragraph. The cause of the deficiency will allow management to decide what, if any, corrective action is appropriate. Subsequently, the standard price report is used by management as a follow-up to see that the corrective action has been taken.

SUMMARY

In many businesses the cost accounting system's greatest value is in revenue control. In these cases, designing a report indicating out-of-line selling prices to management should be considered. A standard selling price report, when properly prepared and analyzed, can be a more effective tool for management action than the traditional product-line profit statements.

CHAPTER ELEVEN

Evaluating a Control System

This book has been concerned with procedures and techniques in cost accounting, cost analysis and budgetary control. Up to this point, each of these techniques and procedures has been treated separately; when taken together, however, they form the basis for an entire control system for short-term (one year or less) management decisions. The purpose of this chapter is to consider the over-all evaluation of a control system.

The procedure for evaluating an existing system is, to some extent, the same as the procedure for establishing a new system. In many respects, developing a new system presents fewer problems than changing an existing system because it is not necessary to overcome the usual resistance to change. In other respects, however, a new system is more difficult, particularly in the implementation stage. Complete new procedures must be developed for all of the accounting and budgeting activities; whereas in an established system many procedures can be retained with little, if any, change. Most new businesses require only a simple cost accounting and budgetary control system in the beginning; therefore, a complicated control system developed from scratch is unusual. For this reason, the chapter is concerned with evaluating an existing control system.

Although the evaluation of a control system is a matter of individual judgment, some general procedures and principles may be applied. This chapter outlines such procedures and principles. (It should be understood, however, that the individual circumstance will always dictate the specific procedure to be used.) The chapter is divided into two parts: (1) evaluating an existing control system; and (2) some general rules for revising a control system.

EVALUATING AN EXISTING CONTROL SYSTEM

Analyzing the Existing System

The first task in evaluating a cost accounting and budgetary control system is to analyze the existing system. A suggested five-step procedure for doing this is explained below.

1. LEARN ABOUT THE COMPANY

The first step in analyzing a control system is to learn as much as possible about the company and, particularly, about the operating decisions that must be made at each level of management. This step is the *sine qua non* of evaluating a control system. Evaluating a control system in the abstract is impossible. The evaluation can be made only within the context of a specific situation. In my experience, the largest single reason for consultants failing to give clients adequate advice on cost and budgetary control has been their failure to understand the company and its problems before recommending revisions to the control system.

Although there are no hard-and-fast rules that cover learning about a company, three areas that must be covered in considerable detail are: marketing, production (in a manufacturing company), and organization. In addition, the greater the familiarity with other areas of the company, the better it will be. (The restriction to learning about a company is, of course, the amount of time available.)

Listed below is the principal information that should be obtained about a company before proceeding with the analysis of its control system.

Marketing. In the marketing area, find out about:
a. The principal *products sold,* including their physical nature, volume of sales and sources of distribution.
b. The factors determining both the *total market* and the *company's share* of that market.
c. The extent to which management can take independent *pricing action.*

d. The extent to which management can influence the *mix of sales*.
e. The extent to which management can *change the design* of the products.
f. The *selling expense* by type of expenditure.

Production. In the production area, find out about:

a. The principal *fabricated products* and the extent of fabrication (that is, value added).
b. The principal *production processes*.
c. The amount of *direct material costs* and the extent to which these costs are controllable.
d. The amount of *direct labor* expense, the extent to which industrial engineering standards are (or can be) used, and the restrictions (either because of union, management policy or production processes) upon its variability.
e. The amount and nature of the *manufacturing overhead* costs.

Organization. In the organization area, find out about:

a. The *nature* of the organization and the *decisions* made at each level.
b. The competency of the *accounting personnel*.
c. The competency of other *key people*. (This may not always be possible.)
d. The nature of the research and development activities and the amount of money being spent in this area.
e. The amount of money being spent on administrative and staff functions, by type of activity.

2. FIND OUT WHAT PROBLEMS THE COMPANY IS FACING

The second step in analyzing a control system is to ascertain the major problems facing the company. This step is particularly important when a company is not earning a satisfactory profit. In general, a company will examine its control system only when profits are unsatisfactory. As a result, in many cases the evaluation of a control system also involves analyzing the reasons for a profit deficiency. Where a profit deficiency exists, the reasons for it should be determined before proceeding with the evaluation of the system because:

a. Management may be relying on the revised control system to solve its problems. If the control system is not an important factor in causing the low profits, management must understand this as soon as possible so that other action may be taken.
b. The cause of the low profits may point up deficiencies in the control system.
c. Short-term corrective action may be necessary; whereas, if the

company were earning a satisfactory profit, it might be more desirable to take action requiring a longer time to implement.

3. FIND OUT HOW UNIT COSTS ARE CALCULATED AND USED

The third step in analyzing a control system is to study the cost accounting system to find out how unit costs are calculated and used. In particular, find out whether the unit costs provide management with the information needed for making intelligent revenue decisions. (Revenue decisions involve selling prices, volume of sales, mix of sales, or products offered for sale.) This step is very important because *most cost accounting systems do not provide adequate data for revenue decisions.*

Unit costs are calculated for three reasons: (1) inventory valuation; (2) cost control; and (3) revenue decisions. The original *raison d'être* for cost accounting was inventory valuation. (This was required in the preparation of the balance sheet and the income statement.) In many companies this is still the major use for unit costs. The reason why many cost accounting systems do not provide adequate data for revenue decisions is that the cost accountant gives primary consideration to developing unit costs for inventory valuation, the least important use from a management point of view. As a result, the cost accounting system is frequently not effective in providing more important information. In those systems where inventory valuation is not given primary consideration, it is usual to develop the system to provide cost control. (This is true of the typical standard cost system.) The unusual cost accounting system is one developed primarily to assist management in making revenue decisions.

In my opinion, the *most important* use of the unit costs developed from an accounting system is to provide information for *revenue decisions.* Yet, this use is given the least (if any) consideration. Many cost accounting systems can be significantly improved by simply deciding the kind of unit cost information that management needs to make revenue decisions and adjusting the system accordingly.

In evaluating a cost accounting system, therefore, the first question to ask is whether management needs unit costs for making revenue decisions. If they are needed, find out exactly what kind of unit costs will provide the best information and how often these costs need to be revised. (Frequently, standard costs adjusted only once a year are all that is necessary.)

At this point, the extent to which unit costs are necessary for cost control should be decided. The effectiveness of the information for revenue decisions should not be subordinated to the cost control aspects without careful consideration. Unit costs, at best, have limited value in cost control. It is important, therefore, not to give up useful information for revenue decisions in order to obtain questionable cost control information.

For example, a company installed a standard cost system that provided for material costs to be based on the estimated prices that would be in effect during the year. Material prices were subject to considerable fluctuations and the company tried to change the selling prices to reflect the changes in material costs. The unit costs, however, did not reflect the changes in material prices because the standards were held constant. The sales manager did his best to keep track of material cost changes so that prices could be adjusted properly. When the cost accountant was asked why he did not reflect actual material cost levels in the unit costs, he replied that standard material costs were necessary for control purposes. (As explained in Chapter 10, a standard cost system does not provide a control over material costs and, in this case, there was practically nothing that the company could do to influence the level of material prices.) The cost accountant had sacrificed the advantage of providing the sales department with unit cost information needed for pricing purposes and in return had provided an illusory control over material costs.

If the unit costs are adequate for revenue decisions and do not interfere with cost control, the next step is to decide whether these unit costs are acceptable for inventory valuation. (Notice that this is precisely the opposite procedure from that normally used. Typically, the inventory valuation is given the primary consideration.) If, for some reason, the unit costs are not acceptable for inventory valuation (by either the certified public accountant or the Internal Revenue Service), the best solution is generally to adjust the inventory values once a year (as when direct costing is employed) for use on the annual statements and tax reports.

Another point to consider about unit costs is whether calculating them (or variances in a standard cost system) monthly is necessary. Frequently, only an annual calculation will be required. If unit costs are not used for revenue purposes (or if standard costs adjusted annually are sufficient) and if cost control is accomplished through budgets, there may be no necessity of going through the expense of allocating costs to department and product more than once a year. Furthermore, not all companies need unit costs. If the unit cost reports are not used by management, perhaps the whole system can be simplified to the point of eliminating most of the cost accounting information. It has been my experience that much cost accounting data could be eliminated with no effect on management's ability to make correct decisions. Recognizing where information is unnecessary is nearly as important as recognizing where necessary information is not being provided.

4. ANALYZE THE COST CONTROL SYSTEM

The fourth step is to analyze the system of cost control. This can be accomplished as follows:

a. List all the categories of costs (for example, material, labor, overhead and so forth) in order of their importance. (The amounts will already have been obtained as part of step 1.)
b. Separate the operating costs from the programmed costs.
c. Examine each of the operating costs and decide the proportion of each that is controllable on a short-term basis.
d. List the controllable operating expenses in order of their importance. Find out how each of these expenses is controlled. Decide how effective these controls are. Pay particular attention to the quality of the cost standards, the methods for flexible budgeting, the adequacy of the reporting system, and the effectiveness of the control system for motivating line management.
e. List each of the programmed costs in the order of its importance. Find out how each of these items is controlled. In particular, examine the procedure for reviewing and approving the amounts to be spent.

5. EXAMINE THE COMMUNICATION SYSTEM

The final step is to learn how management obtains information for decision-making. The formal communication will come from reports and oral presentations. In addition, however, in most companies management receives a considerable amount of information through informal channels, and it is important to know the extent of this.

The following is a procedure for analyzing the communication system:

a. Obtain copies of all reports that management receives. See if these reports provide useful information, if they are complete (for example, answer questions that the information in the report raises), and if the format is adapted to management's use. Be sure to determine whether the information is provided on a selective basis or whether management is being given *all* of the information accumulated by the accounting department. (This is a very common mistake.)
b. Find out what information is provided to management in formal oral presentations.
c. To the extent possible, determine the information that management receives regularly through informal communication channels.

Deciding on the Changes to Be Made

After the control system has been analyzed, the next task is to decide upon the changes that should be made. Much of the information required for this will be obtained during the analytical process. In fact, the process of analyzing a system is largely one of deciding what changes should be made. Nevertheless, it is usually desirable to treat the problem of revising a system separately from the process of analysis. First, the specific changes that should be made in a system cannot be determined (except for those most obvious) until the entire system has been studied and evaluated. Second, all revisions should be directed toward setting up a new, integrated system. Before any specific revisions are decided upon, therefore, the new system should have been determined, at least in general outline.

The following general procedure may be useful in deciding what changes should be made:

1. Decide specifically what financial information management needs for making the day-to-day decisions.
2. Decide what financial information management needs for general background and knowledge (as contrasted to information needed for making decisions).
3. Determine what information is provided by the present system. (This will have been done as part of the analysis.)
4. From the above decide what information management needs but is not getting. Decide which of this information it is practicable to obtain.
5. Decide what information management is now receiving that is not required. Decide which of this information should be eliminated. (Particularly, confusing or conflicting information should be eliminated and information that, though harmless, is expensive to obtain.)

In other words, a good control system will provide management with all of the information that they need for managing the business. At the same time, unnecessary or redundant reports will be eliminated.

SOME GENERAL RULES FOR REVISING A CONTROL SYSTEM

Discussed below are 10 general rules for revising a cost accounting and budgetary control system. In the author's opinion, most unsuccessful attempts to revise existing control systems result from the failure to observe one or more of these rules.

1. The Simplest System Is the Best

Other things being equal, the simplest control system is the best. Many companies do not need complex control systems. To complicate a control system needlessly is not only an expensive practice but, frequently, the information received by management is *worse* than if the system were more simple. One of the most common mistakes made by consultants in installing a system of cost accounting and budgetary control is to make the system more complex and sophisticated than is required for effective control. After deciding upon a control system, therefore, go over each part to see whether it is absolutely necessary and, if necessary, whether it cannot be simplified in some way.

2. Do Not Forget Informal Communication

A mistake frequently made in installing a control system is to forget that in most companies a great deal of informal communication exists. It is surprising how often the accountant or systems analyst will assume that the only information management receives is through the reports that he (the accountant) designs. In developing a reporting system, it is necessary to determine the kind and amount of informal communication that exists and to design the reporting system to take full advantage of this communication.

A typical overhead budget reporting system can be used to demonstrate this point. In an overhead budget system, the systems analyst frequently provides for reporting budget variances to management as soon as possible after the end of the month. (This could be expensive in overtime, for instance.) The reason given for the haste is that management must be informed of off-standard conditions so that prompt corrective action may be taken. This reasoning is all right *if* management needs the report to take corrective action. In most cases, however, if anything is seriously wrong at the plant, management will know about it immediately and take whatever corrective action is required at the time. The report merely provides, on a formal basis, the actual cost of the condition. To be sure, the report is useful in evaluating the performance of the line manager. It is not useful, however, as a basis for immediate corrective action; the informal communication system has already taken care of this. In this example, the difference between publishing the report eight days after the end of the month versus ten days is not worth any additional money.

3. All Control Systems Should Be Tailor-Made

Another common error in systems installation is to install a more or less identical system in two or more companies. The reasoning appears to be that since the system works in Company A, it must be a good system for Company B. It seems to the author that just the opposite is true; the fact that Company A uses a particular system is reason to believe that a different system (or some variation) is required in Company B because all companies are different.

Even if two companies make the same product, it does not follow that they should have identical systems of control. Differences in the abilities and the personalities of the managements would, in itself, dictate some differences in the control system, for example. Another point is that any revised system should be developed to take maximum advantage of the present system. If the present systems are not identical (and they usually are not), the revised systems should probably be different for this reason alone.

4. A Standard Cost System Does Not Automatically Mean that Costs Are Controlled

The existence of a standard cost system does not mean necessarily that a company has an adequate cost control system. As explained in Chapter 10, most standard cost systems do not provide a control over material prices. Furthermore, overhead costs are controlled only if spending variance is separated from volume variance. To do this effectively, an overhead budget is necessary and the budget, not the standard cost system, provides the cost control. Even in the case of direct labor, a standard cost system will usually be effective only if the direct labor standards are based on industrial engineering studies. Also, the fact that a company is meeting its standard costs does not mean that its costs are competitive. Most standard costs are based on existing facilities; if facilities are obsolete, actual costs can be out of line with competition even though they are equal to or better than the standards.

5. Impractical Recommendations Are Useless

Never recommend changes in the control system that cannot be implemented. Not only are the recommendations useless, but the alternative actions are obscured. This situation commonly occurs when a system is developed that requires several highly competent analysts to make it effective. Such a system is not practical where the necessary people are not available or where management has already indicated that it does not intend to add new staff personnel. Recommended changes in a control system should always take into consideration existing restraints. (This does not mean, however, that an attempt should not be made to modify the restraints.)

6. Remember That Change Is Painful

Change is painful for many people because it requires learning to do something differently. There should, therefore, be positive reasons for changing any part of the existing control system. (The change should have a reasonable chance of resulting in increased profits, either directly or indirectly.)

One of the most common examples of unnecessary change concerns changing the format of existing reports. A systems analyst may find that certain reports are confusing and, consequently, he redesigns them to make them more clear *to him*. In doing so, however, he may have made them much worse for management, which is accustomed to working with the present forms and finds them perfectly adequate.

7. People, Not Reports, Make a Control System Effective

One fallacy held by some managers (and, unfortunately, some systems analysts) is that an inadequate control system can be made adequate by redesigning the reports. There may be occasions where this is true, but I am not familiar with any. Usually, a control system will not be an effective management tool without considerable analysis of the data prior to its being submitted to management. If a company has no cost or budget analysts, it will have to develop them from present personnel or hire them from outside the company. Most control systems will not operate without them.

A common practice is to hire a consultant to devise and install a control system. When the consultant leaves, the company has the system but no one to make it work effectively. Few control systems will work without adequate analytical effort and the development of people capable of providing this effort is one of the most important aspects of installing a control system.

8. A Control System Is Not a Panacea for Poor Management

Most companies do not normally consider changing their control systems until they begin experiencing financial problems. It is frequently easy to assume that the lack of control procedures has caused the problems. This may be true in some cases. In many cases, however, the lack of an adequate control system (together with inadequate profits) is symptomatic of inadequate management. Under these conditions, a revised control system might help the company, but it certainly will not solve its problems. A control system will provide only better information to management. Management must be able to make intelligent decisions from this information if the revised control system is to be effective. If management is not capable of making the best decisions, additional information will not be particularly useful.

9. Be Realistic about Timetables

The revision of a cost accounting and budgetary control system is usually no small task. Literally thousands of minor details must be resolved. People must be trained both to develop the information and to use it. Do not make the mistake of assuming that these things can be done overnight. When preparing a timetable, remember many things will almost surely go wrong. As a rule of thumb, it is well to assume that a control system will take twice as long to install as the initial timetable shows. It is better to have management forewarned as to the timing than to have them anticipating that the system will be installed much sooner than it actually will.

10. Plan the System with the Future in Mind

Remember that most companies are constantly growing and changing. Any control system should, to the extent practical, anticipate this growth. It is a difficult and expensive job to change the control system of a company and one that should not be undertaken annually. To minimize the number of changes to the control system, one that will not be quickly outgrown should be developed. In revising the control system, therefore, not only the present situation should be considered but also the probable future changes.

SUMMARY

This chapter has covered the problems of evaluating a cost accounting and budgetary control system. The first step in this process is to analyze the existing system. More than a technical competence in accounting and budgetary control is necessary for this. An understanding of management's problems is required before an intelligent evaluation can be made.

To decide what changes should be made, both the information management needs to make intelligent decisions and the information management receives from both formal and informal sources should be ascertained. The difference between these provides a basis for determining the necessary changes to the system.

Profit Planning [1]

By Marshall K. Evans

The need for new concepts and techniques of profit planning is felt in many companies today. It is true that we have good financial tools for the planning and control of receivables, inventories, and capital facilities, but these tools alone are not enough.

Without more techniques we are handicapped in dealing with the many trends and cross trends which beset modern industry—increasing sales volume but, on the other hand, falling profit margins, expanding investments in capital facilities, growing cost requirements for product and market development, declining return on investment, and so forth.

The problem is likely to be especially acute in areas such as the electrical industry where expansion has been very rapid. Earnings, the ultimate goal of long-range planning, too easily become the victim of the unbridled growth of different corporate functions.

THE PROFIT PATTERN

Something more than good conventional accounting practice is, therefore, required. Management needs improved ways of dealing with what I

[1] Reprinted from the *Harvard Business Review,* July-August, 1959.

shall call the profit pattern of a company or division—its profitability over a period of time, taking into account the particular circumstances and conditions. More specifically:

> How can we evaluate the strong and weak points in the profit pattern of a division to establish objectives that are pinpointed to the organization's needs?
>
> How can we compare the financial effects of alternative courses of action designed to improve the basic profit pattern?
>
> How can we report the effects of different influences on the profit pattern in order to learn whether objectives are being accomplished and, if not, what changes to make in the plan of action?

In this article I shall show how one company, the Westinghouse Electric Corporation, has answered these questions. Some parts of Westinghouse's solution may be familiar to readers, some parts may not. But the combination of techniques and ideas used is, we believe, an original one, and it is proving helpful to management in its efforts to improve the turnover of assets, profit margins, and return on investment.

SEGREGATING COSTS

In the analysis of the profit pattern at Westinghouse, the first step is a vital one. This is to segregate costs and expenses into categories according to the manner in which they respond to short-term changes in the volume of sales. This approach results in three basic cost categories—(1) product costs, (2) committed costs, and (3) managed costs.

Product Costs

The costs which respond directly to changes in the level of production and sales are product costs. These include:

Cost of labor which goes directly into manufacture of the product.

Cost of material which becomes part of the product.

Factory and other overhead costs which are closely allied with production, such as indirect product materials, shop supplies, and some elements of indirect shop labor.

Product costs typically will vary directly with the volume of production and sales, assuming that management has perfect control data, that the mix of production is constant, and that the hourly wage rates and material prices remain unchanged.

Committed Costs

Any costs which remain fixed, over the short term, regardless of the level of production, are committed costs. They are associated primarily with costs of capital facilities such as depreciation charges, insurance, taxes, and rental charges for building and equipment. Over the longer range, these costs will inevitably vary as the result of changes in depreciation policies, the addition and retirement of assets, changes in insurance, and tax rates; but they do *not* respond to fluctuations in volume within the limits of existing facilities.

Managed Costs

All other elements of general overhead expenses are managed costs. The distinguishing characteristic of these costs is that they are subject to management control. For purposes of profit pattern analysis, they may be divided into two subclasses:

1. *Policy costs*—These are dependent almost entirely on management evaluation and judgment and include such items as expenditures for advertising and for research on new products, new methods, and procedures. Such judgment expenditures may vary widely without any immediate effect or relationship to sales volume.

2. *Operating costs*—Here we include the cost of services and processes over and beyond direct product costs—outlays essential to day-to-day business operation but subject to considerable management judgment as to amount and extent. Examples are expenditures for management and supervisory personnel; factory-related manufacturing services for production planning, purchasing, and quality control; general services such as accounting, industrial relations, and order service.

Managed costs may be considered fixed in relationship to production or sales volume, within limits; they respond primarily to management judgment and decision rather than to volume stimuli.

Although significant changes in the volume of production and sales will ultimately bring pressure to increase or decrease the level of managed costs, a fairly wide range of activity can be satisfied without changing the expenditure level. Since the functions covered by managed costs are generally staffed by salaried personnel, short-term expansion or reduction of work in response to short-term changes in the level of production activity is both impractical and undesirable.

GRAPHIC ANALYSIS

In line with these concepts, the profit pattern may be expressed graphically in a fashion similar to a breakdown chart (see Exhibit 1). Since we have defined committed costs and managed costs as being "fixed" with relation to short-term fluctuations in volume, they may be treated, for the purpose of profit-pattern visualization, as constant over the full-volume range. However, product costs by definition vary directly with volume, and are treated as a variable in direct ratio to the number of units produced. The margin between the sales dollar and the product cost per sales dollar contributes to the absorption of managed and committed costs up to the breakeven point, beyond which the margin represents incremental profit.

The important measurements in evaluating the soundness of a particular profit pattern include: ratio of product cost to sales, gross margin over product cost contributed by sales, dollar level of managed and committed costs to be absorbed by gross margin or incremental profit rate, dollar level of the breakeven point, and relationship between actual or projected billings and breakeven point.

Thus, a given division may be producing inadequate profits because:

(1) Margin between product cost and sales price is too narrow, indicating the need for product cost reduction, a price increase, or both.

(2) Committed and managed costs are too high relative to the level of sales or to the production capacity of the facilities and the organization.

(3) Actual sales volume is too low relative to the breakeven point and the capacity of the plant to break into the profit range.

(4) Not *enough* is being spent upon managed costs—say, advertising or quality control services—to generate profitable volume.

UNDERSTANDING THE CAUSES

Up to this point, the profit pattern analysis principle may appear to be only slightly different from the typical breakeven concept. Except for variations in terminology the *concepts* of profit pattern and breakeven charts are in fact basically the same.

Interpretation

The real difference develops in the concepts which are applied to the *interpretation* of the profit pattern. The pattern itself is seen as a first step only—an indispensable one, but in need of a follow-up. It purports to give only a picture of the condition of a division at a particular point in time.

Furthermore, it is applicable only to a relatively limited range of volume change, beyond which the basic management decisions going into the establishment of a level of managed costs must be re-examined.

Inasmuch as development of a profit pattern does only half the job which needs to be done to develop a meaningful dynamic planning tool, we must move on to the job of understanding the causes.

EXHIBIT 1. PROFIT PATTERN:

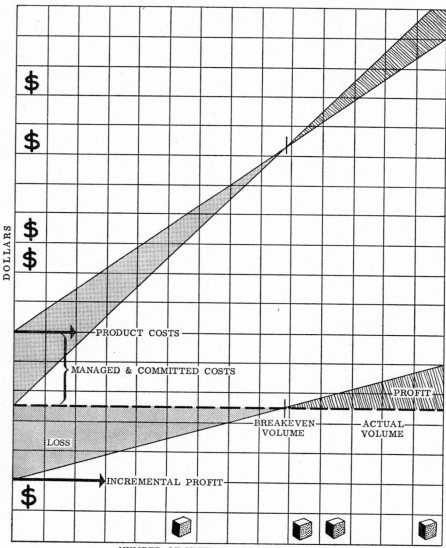

NUMBER OF UNITS PRODUCED AND SOLD

Changes Over Time

Many factors can cause the picture to change between two points in time. For example:

(1) Hourly and salary rates may change as a result of contract negotiations, management policy decisions, merit increases, or changing composition of the work force with relation to length of service.

EXHIBIT 2. SAMPLE FORM:

WESTINGHOUSE FORM 3151 8C

ANALYSIS OF CHANGES IN PROFIT PATTERN — FORM 2

Division: Transmotor Department: ___ Date: 4-1-59 Period: 1958 TO 1960

(DOLLARS IN THOUSANDS)

STMT. LINE NO.	DESCRIPTION	(A) 1958 ACTUAL	(B) MIX CHANGES	(C) GENERAL PAYROLL ADJUST.	(D) DIVISION PAYROLL & MATL. INCR.	(E) POLICY CHANGES	(F)	(G)	(J) REQUIRED COST & EXP. REDUCTIONS	(K) REVISED PATTERN MGMT. CONT.	(L) PRICE CHANGES	(M) PHYSICAL VOLUME	(N) 1960 PROPOSED	(O) 1959 OBJECTIVE	(P) 1957 ACTUAL	FORM 2 LINE NO.
8	GROSS SALES BILLED	12 500								12 500	+500	+1 500	14 500	13 000	12 725	1
9	PRODUCT COSTS - LABOR	2 025	- 75	+ 136					- 104	1 982		+ 210	2 222	1 976	2 163	2
10	• MATERIAL	4 375	- 150		+ 169				- 132	4 262		+ 510	4 772	4 398	4 454	3
11	• FACTORY EXPENSE	1 100	- 35	+ 25	+ 18				- 22	1 086		+ 130	1 216	1 110	1 018	4
12	• OTHER	625		+ 5	+ 26				- 13	643		+ 77	720	638	636	5
13																6
14	TOTAL PRODUCT COSTS	8 125	- 260	+ 166	+ 213				- 271	7 973		+ 957	8 930	8 122	8 271	7
17	COMMITTED COSTS	500		+ 14						514		+ 10	524	507	485	8
18	ORGANIZATION & OTHER OPERATING	900		+ 50		- 45			- 35	900			900	910	940	9
19	FACILITIES PROGRAM EXPENSE	30			+ 30	- 5				35		+ 25	60	35	25	10
20	MANUFACTURING DEVELOPMENT	55			+ 5					60		+ 20	80	60	60	11
21																12
22	DIVISION MANAGED COSTS - MANUFACTURING	985		+ 50	+ 40	- 15			- 35	995		+ 15	1 010	1 005	1 025	13
23	CUSTOMER ORDER DEVELOPMENT - ENGINEERING	250	- 50	+ 13	- 6					207			207	215	260	14
24	STANDARD DEVELOPMENT - ENGINEERING	325		+ 17	+ 8				- 15	335		+ 50	385	370	330	15
25	LONG RANGE MAJOR DEVELOPMENT	70			+ 5	- 50				30			30	40	70	16
26	STANDARD DEVELOPMENT - TOOLS	95		+ 5	+ 10					105		+ 25	130	100	100	17
27																18
28	DIVISION MANAGED COSTS - PROD. DEVELOP.	740		+ 35	+ 17	- 50			- 15	677		+ 75	752	725	760	19
29	DIVISION ADVERTISING	100			+ 5					105		+ 50	155	120	95	20
30	DIVISION & REGION SALES - DIVISION CONT.	400		+ 21	+ 10	- 40				391		+ 20	411	385	395	21
31	DIVISION ORDER SERVICE, WHSE. & SHIPPING	125		+ 5	+ 3					133		+ 5	138	130	120	22
32																23
33	DIVISION MANAGED COSTS - MARKETING	625		+ 26	+ 18	- 40				629		+ 75	704	635	610	24
34	ADMIN. & GENERAL - DIVISION CONTROL	280		+ 15	+ 7	- 25				277			277	264	270	25
35	FOREIGN LIC...ROYALTIES & PAT.CAN.-W INC.	* 5								* 5			* 5	* 5		26
36	OTHER INCOME & DEDUCTIONS - NET	* 15			+ 7					* 15			* 15	* 15	* 10	27
38	DIVISION MANAGED - ADMIN. & GENERAL	260		+ 15	+ 7	- 25				257			257	244	260	28
39	TOTAL DIVISION CONTROL MANAGED COSTS	2 610	- 50	+ 126	+ 82	- 160			- 50	2 558		+ 195	2 753	2 609	2 655	29

184

		+ 310	- 306	- 295	+ 160		+ 321		+500	+ 338				
39b MARGIN OVER DIVISION CONTROL COSTS	1 265							1 455	+500		2 293	1 762	1 314	30
39c MARGIN - % GSB	10.1%							11.6%			15.8%	13.6%	10.3%	31
40 INTERNATIONAL SALES, ADMIN. & GENERAL	25							25			25	25	25	32
41 HEADQUARTERS GENERAL CONTROL EXPENSE	300				+ 28			328			328	310	290	33
42 REG. SALES (APP., DIV.) DIST., SERVICES	300				+ 40			340			340	305	295	34
43 HEADQUARTERS RESEARCH & DEVELOPMENT	100							100			100	100	90	35
45 TOTAL NON-DIVISION MANAGED COSTS	725				+ 68			793			793	740	700	36
46 TOTAL COMMITTED & MANAGED COSTS	3 855							3 865			4 070	3 856	3 840	37
47 INVENTORY CHANGE - EFFECT ON IBT	* 50				50						* 75	* 25	20	38
48 INCOME BEFORE TAXES	490	+ 310	- 306	- 295	+ 142		+ 321	662	+500	+ 413	1 575	997	634	39
49 IBT AS % GSB	3.9%							5.3%			10.9%	7.7%	5.0%	40
50 BREAKEVEN VOLUME	10 957							10 671			10 596	10 277	10 971	41
51 BREAKEVEN VOLUME - % GSB	87.7%							85.4%			73.1%	79.1%	86.2%	42
52 INCREMENTAL IBT RATE	.3500							.3622			.3841	.3752	.3500	43
2 GROSS ASSETS	7 500							7 500			8 290	7 700	7 650	44
1 % RETURN ON GROSS ASSETS	6.4%							8.7%			19.0%	12.9%	8.3%	45

* CONTRA OR LOSS

185

(2) Selling prices may change.

(3) In a multiproduct division, the mixture of products with different margins over product costs may vary, with resultant change in the total contribution to absorption of managed and committed costs and to the over-all dollar level of income.

(4) Policy decisions by management may result in changed levels of expenditure for policy costs, different approaches to organization structure, and in different concepts of the type of service deemed necessary for design, production, and selling, and for employee and community relations.

(5) New plant investments, purchases of additional capital equipment, retirement of worn-out and obsolete equipment, and changed tax regulations may result in changes in committed cost levels for depreciation, insurance, and taxes.

(6) Prices of purchased materials may change upward or downward, resulting in fluctuations in the product costs per unit.

(7) Changes in the product design may result in higher or lower product cost content per unit.

(8) Improvements in manufacturing methods, automation, and other areas can reduce the product cost content, while at the same time increase committed or managed costs for depreciation, maintenance, and so on.

(9) Changing levels of productivity effort on the part of employees in the shop and office can affect favorably or adversely the levels of both product costs and managed costs.

(10) Improvement of systems and methods in the office operations, including the mechanization of clerical procedures, can bring about reductions in managed costs.

If a clear understanding of the causes for profit variation over past periods is to be developed, it is necessary to isolate and evaluate the effect of the influencing factors. Also, if we want to know what action to take to improve profits in the future, we must have good estimates of the effect of different critical factors in the future. And we must be able to set appropriate objectives for accomplishing improvements which are within the over-all control of management.

In other words, a picture of a company's or a division's operation at a particular point in time is not enough. A sound planning procedure must also take into account the influence of different factors on the organization as it goes from one period to another.

Analysis Form

The development of profit pattern analyses in Westinghouse divisions is expressed in a profit pattern analysis form. Exhibit 2 shows a sample for the "Transmotor Division" (disguised):

Beginning and ending profit patterns are recorded in the first and last columns of the form.

Past trends are analyzed by comparing the profit patterns for two historical years and then developing the influencing factors in the intervening columns.

Future plans are laid by recording in the first column the latest available profit pattern, establishing the objective pattern toward which the division plans to work, and forecasting the effect of influencing factors in between.

Typically the procedure requires entering the expected effects of general wage and material cost changes, and developing by difference the amount of improvement through cost and expense reduction necessary to obtain the desired levels.

Basic Tools

I should emphasize here that certain basic tools must be maintained in order to provide accurately the information that is ultimately carried to the profit pattern analysis. For example:

Continuing indexes of selling prices, labor rates, and purchased material prices should be kept so that management can calculate the relative impact of these changing factors for any given level of production and sales volume.

All Westinghouse divisions maintain formalized cost reduction programs, in which the design and manufacturing, sales, and purchasing engineers study each product, subassembly, and component for the purpose of devising less expensive features, improving manufacturing methods, and utilizing less expensive materials in order to produce a high quality product at a minimum cost.

Organization analysis and planning, as well as office systems and methods analyses, contribute to increased productivity of managed-cost personnel.

The margin over product costs contributed by individual product lines is developed as the basis for review of pricing decisions and policies and for pruning out unprofitable products which cannot, within a relatively short period of time, be placed on a profitable basis through either cost reduction or price revisions.

INFLUENCE FACTORS

The key to useful profit pattern analyses lies in the accurate development of the factors that influence results. These fall broadly into two categories: (1) those which are primarily internal and/or subject to management control, and (2) those which are heavily influenced by external market conditions and competition.

Subject to Control

In the first category, the principal factors are: changes in wage and salary rates, material prices, mix of product lines, decisions to spend or withhold spending in policy areas, and cost and expense reduction accomplishments:

The effect of changes in wage rates is calculated from the provisions of existing labor contracts or from forecasts based on management's objectives in negotiations of new contracts.

To obtain the effect of material prices, it is necessary to keep accurate indexes of past material prices, and to predict the trend of these indexes for the principal types of raw materials and parts purchased. The full dollar impact is developed by applying the forecasted per-unit change to the labor, salary, and material content of the various categories of cost.

The effect of product mix changes can be significant where several product lines are manufactured and sold, and where the margin between product cost and selling price varies from one line to another. A fixed dollar sales volume will be produced at varying product costs depending on the mixture of products involved. This effect is calculated by comparing the product costs for the planned mix with the costs for the actual mix in the base period. The result is increased or decreased cost, depending on whether the mix is unfavorable or favorable.

The cost and expense reduction figures are initially obtained by difference—the difference between the accumulated effect of the other influencing factors and the level of cost and expense required to produce the desired profit result. These figures become the goal for cost and expense reduction during the period involved. They may have to be tempered if the amounts squeezed out by difference are obviously unattainable, resulting also in modification of the profit goal.

External Conditions

Because changes in product selling price and volume are, to a degree, speculative in nature, these are tacked on to the plan after the full effect of the internal influencing factors has been calculated. The objective is to focus maximum attention on profit improvement by internal action, and to avoid too heavy reliance on the external factors in programming for desired profit objectives. This is not to say that programs to improve volume and price realization should not be pushed to the maximum, but rather that expense programming should be done so as to produce a suitable profit at a conservative volume base.

Calculation of the effect of physical volume changes is done by applying the planned product cost ratio to the dollar increase or decrease in sales volume. Required changes in managed cost levels to meet the change in volume are developed by applying the variable elements of budget standards applicable to the various managed cost categories or by management decision as to the level of expenditure needed in marketing areas to produce the planned volume change.

The calculation of the effect of realized price changes can be very simple or extremely difficult, depending on the nature of the product. Where a standard product is involved, application of known or forecasted price changes to the number of units in the volume base will produce the total dollar effect. But in product lines in which units are designed and manufactured to customer specifications, every unit is different and prices are not comparable. In these cases, the calculated effect of price changes is much less precise. The problem may be approached by detailed analysis of cost/price factors for a representative style of product, or an answer may be calculated from a "quoted margin" base, rather than from a total price base.

In any case, even a crude answer is better than no answer at all, and the necessity of at least attempting a calculation has pointed up some basic weaknesses in pricing policies and procedures.

REPORTS TO MANAGEMENT

No planning and control procedure is complete without prompt and accurate feedback of operating results. Management must know how actual profit performance compares with the objective and with past performances, and to what extent variations from objective and from past performance have been caused by the various influencing factors indicated.

To meet this need, Westinghouse executives have designed a monthly operating report of the type shown on pp. 192–3 in Exhibit 3 (filled out, again, for the "Transmotor Division"). The actual results for a month and for the period of the year to date are reported in the profit pattern format. Results are compared with the budget or objectives, and the variances from budget are calculated. In addition, the cause of variance from the objective and from a base period in the past are calculated and reported at the bottom of the form.

Within the various operating divisions, the different categories of expense as reported on the profit pattern are supported by detailed budget statements developing actual budgeted expenditures matched against individual control accounts. Also, product line statements are prepared reporting profits by product line in terms of contributed margin and of share of general prorated expenses. These subsidiary reports enable top management to evaluate actual performance on an exception basis and direct corrective action to the appropriate area.

Planning Procedure

What can be done to provide for greater top management participation in setting objectives, for more detailed consideration of basic improvement requirements, and for a closer tie between long-range plans, short-range budgets, and actual results? One helpful step is a new procedure that was developed and put in operation at Westinghouse early in 1957. Experience with it has been extremely favorable, and while small alterations will undoubtedly be made from year to year, it is expected that the basic features of the method will be continued for several years.

The most fundamental change from the procedures formerly used is that planning reviews have been put on a rolling schedule throughout the year. During each month top management reviews the plans and objectives of three to five operating divisions, covering all of the divisions over the 12-month period. This review is attended by the president, executive vice president, other members of corporate top management, the product group general managers, and the vice presidents for sales, engineering, manufacturing, and finance. The division manager is responsible for preparing his plan, reviewing it with his group manager, and then presenting it to the top management committee.

In addition to the profit pattern analysis, the division managers prepare, as part of their presentation to the committee, a five-year projection of market trends for each product line, a forecast of capital facilities requirements, and a projection of working capital requirements for the target year. These projections, together with the profit pattern analysis, are supported by specific plans of action to cope with the particular problems of the division as revealed by the analysis. These action plans may be directed to a reduction of managed costs or product costs, increased sales effort to step up sales volume relative to the breakeven point, shifted emphasis in development to update product designs or increase the speed of developing new products, or modernization or expansion of facilities to meet the requirements of growth or improvement.

Another change in procedure shortens the length of time covered by the planning cycle. Formerly the initial planning called for a fifth-year projection of markets, facilities, and profit margins. But five years, in most of the cases we deal with, is too far in the future for the kind of specific planning called for, and planning so far ahead led to inflation of programs of all kinds tied to long-range market projections. It was decided, therefore, at least for a few years, to focus planning attention on the next full calendar year. To illustrate:

In January 1958, general company goals for improvement of operations were adopted and communicated to the division managers at a management meeting. In February, top management began to review the objective and plans of each division for the year 1959. Subsequently, detailed plans were reviewed in the light of their contribution to the over-all company objectives as well as to the solution of the specific problems which were facing managers.

Finally, the new procedure provides for a better comparison of objectives and results. Both division and corporate managements receive a periodic playback of long-range plans against short-range budgets and against actual performance to date.

This step permits evaluation of planning deficiencies, adjustment of emphasis in planning, and measurement of the planning and operating performance of division managers in terms applicable to each individual situation. It is likely that in future years the length of the planning cycle will be increased, at least for some of those divisions which have long product cycles through booking of orders, design, and manufacture. On the other hand, it is not likely that the longer-range objectives will be disassociated from shorter-range plans and current operating performance.

POINTING UP OPPORTUNITIES

How can profit pattern analysis help management? What kinds of opportunities for improvement can it point up? Westinghouse's experience is a revealing one, and I should like to turn now to some examples of what has been accomplished. It might be argued, of course, that some of these gains might have happened anyway—without profit pattern analysis. It is our conviction, however, that the new approach has revealed problems more clearly and has stimulated prompt and constructive action by management.

Managed-Cost Trends

Confirming pre-existing suspicions, profit pattern analyses revealed that the level and trend of managed costs was unsatisfactory. The analyses not only pointed up the contributing factors, but also provided a means for determining the level to which managed costs should be held

EXHIBIT 3. SAMPLE FORM:

FORM 32311

WESTINGHOUSE ELECTRIC CORPORATION
(INCLUDING INTERNATIONAL COMPANY)
STATEMENT OF OPERATIONS & ANALYSIS OF IBT VARIANCE
19___

MONTH OF ___March, 1959___

STATEMENT 6
PAGE ___
DIV. ___
DEPT. ___

Transmotor

(DOLLARS IN THOUSANDS)

LINE NO.	CURRENT MONTH			SCH NO.	DESCRIPTION	YEAR TO DATE		
	OBJECTIVE	ACTUAL	VARIANCE			VARIANCE	ACTUAL	OBJECTIVE
1	9.3%	5.4% *	* 3.9%		% RETURN ON TOTAL GROSS ASSETS	3.7% *	14.0% *	10.3%
2	7 625	7 595	30		TOTAL GROSS ASSETS	32	7 588	7 620
3	1.5	1.5	-		ASSET TURNOVER	.1	1.6	1.5
4	1 050	1 075	25		ORDERS ENTERED - CUSTOMER	215	3 220	3 005
5	50	55	5		- INTERUNIT	15	135	120
6	2 575	2 610	35		UNFILLED ORDERS - CUSTOMER	35	2 610	2 575
7	150	125 *	25 *		- INTERUNIT	25 *	125	150
8	950	920 *	30 *		GROSS SALES BILLED	110	3 010	2 900
9	142	137	5		PRODUCT COSTS - LABOR	20 *	455	435
10	323	315	8		• MATERIAL	59 *	1 045	986
11	86	82	4		• FACTORY EXPENSE	10 *	242	232
12	57	53	4		• OTHER	20	180	200
14	(608	(587	21		TOTAL PRODUCTS COSTS	69 *	1 922	1 853
15	(342)	(333)	(* 9)		MARGIN OVER PRODUCT COSTS	41	(1 088)	1 047)
16	.3600)	.3613)	(.0013)		MARGIN RATIO TO G.S.B.	.0005	(.3615)	.3610)
17	40	41	1 *		COMMITTED COSTS	2	118	120
18	72	70	2		ORGANIZ. & OTHER OPER.	5	215	220
19	5	10	5		FACILITIES PROGRAM EXP.	-	10	10
20	-	-	-		MFG. DEVELOPMENT	5 *	10	5
22	77	80	3 *		DIVISION MGD. COSTS - MFG.	-	235	235
23	15	14	1		C.O. DEVELOP. - ENGRG.	5	45	50
24	25	22	3		STD. DEVELOP. - ENGRG.	2	70	72
25	3	3	-		LONG RANGE MAJOR DEVELOPMENT	-	9	9
26	5	10	5 *		STD. DEVELOP. - TOOLS	-	10	10
28	48	49	1 *		DIVISION MGD. COSTS - PRODUCT DEVELOPMENT	7	134	141
29	5	10	5 *		DIVISION ADVERTISING	5	15	20
30	30	32	2 *		DIVISION & REGION SALES - DIVISION CONTR.	5	85	90
31	9	8	1		DIVISION ORDER SERV., WHSE. & SHIP.	2	23	25

DIVISION MANAGED COSTS / INCOME BEFORE TAXES statement (figures in thousands / percent of G.S.B.; `*` = unfavorable in variance columns)

Line	Item	Actual	1959 Obj.	Var.	Actual	1959 Obj.	Var.
33	DIVISION MGD. COSTS - MARKETING	50	44	*6	135	123	*12
34	ADM. & GEN'L - DIVISION CONTROL	19	20	1	52	50	2
35	FOR., LIC., ROY. & PAT., CAN. W INC.	—	—	—	—	*2	2
36	OTHER INCOME & DEDUCTIONS - NET	*3	*2	1	*6	*7	1
37							
38	DIVISION MGD. COSTS - ADM. & GEN'L	16	18	*2	46	41	5
39	TOTAL DIV. MANAGED COSTS	195	187	8	557	533	24
40	INT'L SALES, ADM. & GEN'L	4	2	2	6	7	*1
41	HDQTRS. GEN'L CONTROL EXPENSE	26	26	—	78	78	—
42	REGIONAL SALES (APPR. DIV.) & DIST. SER.	25	25	—	75	75	—
43	HDQTRS. RESEARCH & DEVELOPMENT	8	8	—	24	24	—
44							
45	TOTAL NON-DIV. MANAGED COSTS	63	61	2	183	184	*1
46	TOTAL COMM. & MANAGED COSTS	299	288	11	860	835	25
47	INVENTORY CHANGE - EFFECT ON IBT	—	5	*5	10	12	2
48	INCOME BEFORE TAXES	34	59	*25	197	265	*68
49	INCOME BEFORE TAXES - % G.S.B.	3.7%	6.2%	*2.5%	6.8%	8.8%	*2.0%
50	BREAKEVEN VOLUME	828	800	28	2,382	2,309	73
51	BREAKEVEN VOLUME - % G.S.B.	90.0%	84.2%	5.8%	82.1%	76.7%	5.4%

ANALYSIS OF IBT VARIANCE

Line	CAUSE OF VARIANCE	From 1959 Obj.	From 1959 Obj.	Same Period 1958 Actual
53	REALIZED SALES PRICES	20	10	15
54	VOLUME OF G.S.B.	4	36	197
55	MIX OF SALES	12	7	22
56	PRODUCT COSTS - WAGE & MAT'L RATES	*2	3	*52
57	- OTHER	5	5	35
58				
59				
60	MARGIN OVER PRODUCT COSTS	9	41	217
61	COMM., & MGD. COSTS - DIV. - WAGE & MAT'L	1	2	*20
62	- OTHER	*8	28	10
63	ADJUSTMENT FOR INVENTORY CHANGE	*5	2	20
64				
65	TOTAL VARIANCE - DIVISION CONTROL	23	69	207
66	NON-DIVISION - MANAGED COSTS	*2	1	*3
67	- OTHER			
68				
69	TOTAL VARIANCE - IBT	25	68	210

* CONTRA IN COST & EXPENSES
• LOSS ON LINE 48
* UNFAVORABLE IN VARIANCE COLUMNS
SPONSORED BY F. E. DALTON

Courtesy Westinghouse Electric Corporation

if adequate profits were to be earned under various volume conditions. Furthermore, they provided the mechanics for measuring the effect of various alternative management decisions. For example, the cost of a stepped-up program for market penetration could be evaluated in terms of the additional sales volume necessary to overcome the costs of the program and produce a net gain in profitability.

Convincing knowledge of the effect of managed-cost trends and their relative importance in the total cost picture led to an aggressive management drive to contain the growth of these trends. This was done by more careful evaluation of plans to spend money in such judgment areas as product development, sales promotion, advertising, and public relations; by the adoption of formalized industrial engineering techniques for the analysis of paperwork systems and the productivity of nonfactory personnel; also by development of a formalized approach to organization analysis and simplification.

Profit Detractors

A specific program was initiated throughout the corporation for detailed studies of each product line not contributing a normal margin over product costs. Objectives were to determine why the product was not producing adequate margins, what could be done through redesign or improved manufacture to reduce costs, and finally, whenever all alternatives appeared inadequate, to face up to the decision of abandoning that product line. As a result of this approach the loss from these so-called "profit detractors" has been substantially reduced. Several individual product lines have been dropped, and one operating department has been discontinued and its plant disposed of.

In singling out individual product lines for detailed study, courses of action necessary to make them more profitable became obvious very quickly. Before profit pattern analysis these courses of action had been obscured by the fact that the results for individual product lines were lost in general profit and loss figures. Now specific opportunities emerged. Here are some concrete examples:

In some cases it became evident that product cost-selling price relationships were basically good, but sales volume was insufficient to absorb the managed costs associated with the product. This resulted in intensified sales efforts, either through re-alignment of sales responsibility or by the expenditure of more advertising and sales promotional funds.

In other cases it was discovered that overhead organizations had been built in anticipation of larger sales volume than could be realized in the foreseeable future. Management decided, therefore, to scale these managed cost structures down to a size suitable for the volume of sales actually being realized.

Situations were also discovered in which a net improvement in over-all profit margins could be obtained by re-alignment of manufacturing or selling responsibilities for "profit detractor" lines. In one case it was discovered that management responsibility for an individual product had been separated from responsibility for the end product in which the "profit detractor" was a component part. Combining the two responsibilities led to more effective direction of development efforts in the component and to expanded use of the component both in the end product division and in the outside market as well.

Cost-Price Squeeze

The profit pattern analysis has dramatically portrayed the seriousness of the squeeze on profits which has been caused by the upward trend of wage and salary rates and raw material costs, and by the historic reluctance of the electrical industry to translate rising costs into higher prices. It has become clear to all levels of management that, unless the rate of increase in wages is brought into line with the rate of increase in productivity of *all* employees, hourly and salary, either prices must rise or profit margins will continue to suffer; and that management policies must be guided accordingly. For example, we see today that:

(1) The attitude with which management approaches the bargaining table to negotiate contract changes needs to be studied with particular reference to the ability of the company to recover the cost of such wage increases through productivity improvement or price increases.

(2) The whole area of pricing policy and procedures needs to be studied to assure anticipation of contractual increases in costs and to exploit every practical opportunity for assuming price leadership.

Excess Capacity

In a few divisions the profit pattern analyses show that too wide a gap exists between current production levels and the capacity of existing facilities. This gap, for several reasons, makes earning adequate profits virtually impossible despite all efforts to reduce product and managed costs. Accordingly, action has been initiated to step up marketing programs and promotional activities; to increase sales volume relative to the breakeven point; and to reduce excess capacity with its attendant overheads by consolidating production in lower cost location and by closing out or retiring idle or excess plant and equipment.

EXECUTIVE EFFECTIVENESS

To sum up, the profit pattern concept provides for the segregation of income and cost data according to the factors which cause them to change. It provides a means for evaluating the effect on profits of such influencing factors as: price levels, sales volume, mix of product, changing labor and material rates, and cost reductions through redesign and methods improvements.

By segregating the elements of profit performance in these categories, the new concept reveals to management the general lines of approach which must be taken to improve results. Once this is done, specific plans of action and tools for improvement can be utilized, with the profit pattern arrangement facilitating evaluation of various courses of action.

The universal reaction of line managers at Westinghouse, after almost two years of using the profit pattern technique, is that they now have a far better understanding of what is going on in the company and in the various divisions. Consequently, they have been able to plan and carry out programs of action specifically suited to the problems at hand.

Line Fitting

The cost and budget analyst is frequently faced with the necessity of calculating the relationship between two variables. Usually these variables are manufacturing expense and the volume of production (in developing an overhead budget) or profits and the volume of sales (in developing a profit-volume chart). Some of the principal methods for estimating this relationship were explained in Chapters 6 and 9. One of these methods involved fitting a line to historical data. This can be done by plotting the data on a graph and drawing a line through the points by sight. Another method is to calculate the line mathematically. The most common mathematical technique for fitting a line to historical data is called the method of least squares.

THE METHOD OF LEAST SQUARES

The objective in fitting a line to historical data is to draw the line in such a way that the difference between the plotted points and the values indicated by the line are at a minimum. The best fitting line is the one that results in the smallest total when the differences between the plotted point and the line are summed. The deviations will, of course, be both negative and positive; if the actual values of the deviations are used

197

and added algebraically, they might net to a small amount even though the fit of the line were poor. One alternative is to use the absolute value (the value ignoring the sign) of the deviations. Absolute values, however, are inconvenient to work with mathematically. All of the actual deviations can be converted mathematically to a positive sign by squaring them. If the squares of the deviations are used, this eliminates the problem of different signs and, at the same time, provides a more convenient mathematical method. For this reason, the most common method for fitting a line results in establishing an equation for a line where the squares of the deviations of the actual data from the line are minimized. It is for this reason that it is called the method of least squares.

Derivation of the Normal Least-Square Equations [2]

The two least-square equations are as follows:

$$\Sigma y = na + b\Sigma x$$
$$\Sigma xy = a\Sigma x + b\Sigma x^2$$

These equations are derived as follows:

Let y_i = the actual value of y at point x_i, and
y'_i = the value of the fitted line at point x_i

The objective is to keep the square of the errors $\sum_{i=1}^{n}(y_i - y'_i)^2$ to a minimum. But $y'_i = a + bx_i$. Therefore, the square of the errors will be:

$$F(a, b) = \sum_{i=1}^{n}(y_i - a - bx_i)^2$$

To minimize this function:

(1) Take the partial derivative;

$$\frac{\partial F}{\partial a} = \sum_{i=1}^{n} 2(y_i - a - bx_i)(-1)$$

(2) Set the derivative equal to zero;

$$\sum_{i=1}^{n} 2(y_i - a - bx_i)(-1) = 0$$

---

[2] It is not necessary to understand this derivation in order to use and understand the method of least squares. The derivation is included for the interested student. Students with limited mathematical backgrounds should omit this section.

$$\sum_{i=1}^{n}(y_i - a - bx_i) = 0$$

(3) Solve for y.

$$\Sigma y = na + b\Sigma x$$

The second normal equation is obtained by means of the partial derivations with respect to b, as follows:

(1)

$$\frac{\partial F}{\partial b} = \sum_{i=1}^{n} 2(y_i - a - bx_i)([-1][-x_i])$$

(2)

$$\sum_{i=1}^{n} 2(y_i - a - bx_j)(x_i) = 0$$

$$\sum_{i=1}^{n} (x_iy_i - ax_i - bx_i^2) = 0$$

(3)

$$\Sigma xy = a\Sigma x + b\Sigma x^2$$

Calculation of the Line

The line will be determined by the values of a and b. These values are obtained in three steps:

(1) Calculate the values Σx, Σy, Σxy and Σx^2 (Σ simply means "the sum of");
(2) Substitute these values in the normal equations;
(3) Solve the equations for a and b.

1. For each point, record the values of X and Y. The Y will be the value on the vertical scale (profits or costs); the X will be the value on the horizontal scale (sales or production). From these values calculate XY and X^2 for each point and sum the results. For example, the problem is to establish a relationship by the method of least squares between indirect labor and the volume of production, expressed in standard direct labor hours. The relationship between the two during the previous year was as follows:

Month	Indirect Labor Cost	Standard Direct Labor Hours
	(000 omitted)	
January	110	50
February	110	60
March	120	70
April	140	80
May	130	80
June	130	70
July	140	90
August	120	50
September	110	40
October	130	60
November	140	70
December	140	80

The calculation of the values of the variables is as follows:

Y (1) Indirect Labor Cost	X (2) Standard Direct Labor Hours	XY (3) (1 × 2)	X² (4) (2) × (2)
110	50	5,500	2,500
110	60	6,600	3,600
120	70	8,400	4,900
140	80	11,200	6,400
130	80	10,400	6,400
130	70	9,100	4,900
140	90	12,600	8,100
120	50	6,000	2,500
110	40	4,400	1,600
130	60	7,800	3,600
140	70	9,800	4,900
140	80	11,200	6,400
1,520	800	103,000	55,800

Therefore:

$$\Sigma y = 1520$$
$$\Sigma x = 800$$
$$\Sigma xy = 103,000$$
$$\Sigma x^2 = 55,800$$
$$n = 12$$

2. The next step is to substitute the values just calculated for the variables in the normal equations:

(1) $\Sigma y = na + bx$

(2) $\Sigma xy = a\Sigma x + b\Sigma x^2$

Substituting:

   (1) $1,520 = 12a + 800b$

   (2) $103,000 = 800a + 55,800b$

3. The final step is to solve the two simultaneous equations just calculated. The simplest way is usually to eliminate a by subtraction. (This is nothing more than the old high school method.) Either of the equations can be multiplied by any constant and one subtracted from the other. The objective is to multiply both by a constant that will make a in both equations the same and subtract the first equation from the second. This will give you the value of b. By substituting this value in one of the equations, the value of a will be obtained. In this case, multiply the first equation by 200 and the second equation by 3, as follows:

   (1) $304,000 = 2400a + 160,000b$

   (2) $309,000 = 2400a + 167,400b$

Subtracting the first equation from the second and rearranging, we have:

$$7,400b = 5,000; \text{ and}$$
$$b = \frac{5,000}{7,400} = .676$$

Substituting .676 for b in equation (1),

$$304,000 = 2400a + 108,160$$
$$2400a = 195,840$$
$$a = 81.6 \text{ or } 81,600 \text{ (Remember, all calculations are in thousands.)}$$

The relationship of indirect labor to standard direct labor hours is expressed by the following equation:

$y = 81,600 + .676x$, which would probably be rounded off to:
$y = \$80,000 + .68x$.

This equation can also be expressed as follows:

Monthly indirect labor costs $= \$80,000 + \$0.68$ for each standard direct labor hour.

SHORT-CUT METHODS

If a large number of lines are to be fitted by the method of least squares, it might be well to use one of the short-cut ways of making these calculations. *Applied General Statistics*, 2nd edition, by Croxton and Cowden (Englewood Cliffs, N. J.: Prentice-Hall, Inc., 1955) includes a description of several of these methods.

Testing for Statistical Significance

One of the problems that the budget analyst sometimes faces is whether there is a sufficiently direct relationship between cost and the volume of production to treat it on a flexible budgetary basis. If the method of least squares is used to determine the line, the analyst may apply the chi-square test. This test will tell him the probability that the relationship between the cost and volume are not the result of random factors, or, to put it the other way, the probability that the relationship between the cost and volume, as expressed by the equation, represents an actual relationship. The description of the chi-square test and how to use it can be found in nearly every elementary statistical text.

Tests for statistical significance are rarely used in budgeting. If the relationship between the variables is not evident on sight, there is considerable question as to whether any useful relationship exists.

Index